RUST BELT VEGAN KITCHEN

RUST BELT
VEGAN
KITCHEN

Recipes, Resources, and Stories

EDITED BY MEREDITH PANGRACE

Belt Publishing

ISBN: 9781953368119

Belt Publishing
5322 Fleet Avenue
Cleveland, Ohio 44105
www.beltpublishing.com

Cover and book design by Meredith Pangrace

This book is dedicated to the warm kitchen memories that unite us all.

TABLE OF CONTENTS

INTRODUCTION
THE HUMBLE CABBAGE

On New Year's Day, 2021, I was making dinner to take to my parents' house. Due to the pandemic, our holiday plans had diminished to just a few of us casually gathering for an early supper in jeans and sweaters. It had been a year of fear, loneliness, and loss that we were all ready to say goodbye to. So in the hope of lifting spirits and making the meal still feel special, I decided to make a few family favorites, including stuffed cabbage.

My grandmother had shown me years ago how to steam the cabbage leaves—a little boiling water in the pot, loosely covered, slowly peeling off the outer leaves with tongs, one at a time, as they steamed and became soft enough to roll. It was a task that took a quiet patience (in my otherwise chaotic kitchen), and it forced me into a moment of reflection. I thought about how she probably learned this same technique from her mother, a Slovak immigrant who came to southern Ohio more than a century ago. I looked at the veins in the cabbage leaves and they reminded me of my grandma's veined hands and delicate skin. I thought about the cabbage, tough yet humble—a vegetable that was a staple in not just the Eastern European immigrant diet, but in so many other culinary traditions in our region. People of all backgrounds who came to the cities of the Rust Belt for work and were looking for familiar, affordable ingredients to fill their families' bellies relied on cabbage. I thought about how when I stopped eating meat as a teenager, my grandma would roll a few of her cabbage leaves and fill them with only rice, just for me. She didn't understand my choice completely, because to her, eating meat was a privilege. To be able to afford to eat meat, and choose not to, didn't align with the way she was raised. But nevertheless, she didn't judge me, didn't criticize, and she lovingly accommodated my choice with extra servings of potatoes, pasta, and, of course, cabbage when I came for dinner.

Like many of us, during the pandemic, I spent a lot of time in my tiny kitchen experimenting, specifically with making things from scratch that I usually buy—

bean burgers, protein bars, dairy-free cheese, yogurt—because I had the time. I experimented with making plant-based versions of dishes I craved, searching for new ingredients online, watching YouTube instructional videos, scrolling Instagram, and ordering cookbooks. All this culminated in the New Year's Day vegan feast of pierogis, paprikash, stuffed cabbage, mashed potatoes, and noodles.

The meal was worth boasting about on social media, so I shared it. There were a lot of comments—questions about how I modified the recipes, drooling-face emojis, and pictures of dishes other people were creating. Intrigued, I collected the responses and started reaching out to local home chefs and professional chefs who had an interest in vegan food. I asked what they were making and why. Some liked the challenge of a new way of cooking. Some mentioned a passion for animals or the environment. Some mentioned a demand for more plant-based food from their customers. Some mentioned health concerns or allergies.

While the reasons for their invention varies, the recipes in this book all have something in common. These dishes aren't the avocado-and-sprout spa menu meals of the West Coast. The vegan food of the Rust Belt offers comfort and brews nostalgia. The ingredients showcase the diversity, flavors, and history of our region. We love eating local here, but it's not easy. Our recipes focus on what is possible in a place where the growing season is limited and our winters are long and cold. In this book, that means an abundance of winter vegetables like potatoes and squash, and shelf-stable items like pickles, canned pumpkin, and dried mushrooms—but I've included a few showstoppers for those precious few weeks when tomatoes are actually in season. You'll also notice several unpretentious shortcuts, because in true Midwestern fashion, we admit that sometimes we just can't do it all.

I'd like to think this book is for everyone. If you're not familiar with food of the Rust Belt, you'll discover Cincinnati Chili and Cleveland Polish Boys. If you're not vegan, you'll learn how simple it is to bake a cake without eggs or milk. If you're new to plant-based cooking, I hope this book will present it in a more accessible, less challenging light. And if you're a stalwart vegan or vegetarian, much of this may be familiar, but I hope you can get a few new ideas from it and appreciate that your community is growing, even here in the Rust Belt. I want to thank all the chefs in every community who contributed their inventiveness and creativity in coming up with the recipes. Their skills and talents are so appreciated for making this an engaging, diverse and flavor-filled book.

More than anything, this book is not going to criticize you for whatever choices you make in your diet. It will encourage you to open your mind and enter the Rust Belt Vegan Kitchen. Trust us, it's a delicious place to be.

—Meredith Pangrace
Cleveland, Ohio

PANTRY STAPLES

There are a handful of items that are helpful to have on hand in the Rust Belt Vegan Kitchen (RBVK). Most are easy to find in grocery stores, and others can be found online or in ethnic markets. In our region, the summers of fresh vegetables are fleeting, and our winter temperatures often make it unbearable to leave the house, but if you have these items on the shelves along with your standard pantry staples, you won't have any trouble concocting a vegan dinner.

Agar Agar

This is a powder made from seaweed that can be used to make vegan cheese and gummy candies, and to thicken sauces. It's the most difficult item on the list to find, and it's a bit pricey, but if you order a small bag online, it'll last you a long time, as most recipes call for a very small amount.

Black Salt (Kala Namak)

Visit a local Indian market if you're having trouble finding this sulphurous-smelling salt. Adding this to your tofu scramble, chickpea flour omelet, or the viral Tabitha Brown vegan deviled "eggs" will give the dish that eggy flavor you might be missing. Try using it as a replacement for regular salt in the Breakfast Scramble (p. 30).

Chickpeas (Canned)

The humble salad bar garnish has been elevated in status to the star of the RBVK pantry. (Need convincing? Try the Dumplings with Gravy recipe on p. 130.) Fork-mashed, they become the replacement for tuna salad. Pulverize them with other vegetables and spices to make sliders. Toss them into stews and pastas for fiber, protein, and texture. Roast them in the oven for a salty snack. The possibilities are endless. Some cooks prefer to buy them dried to soak and then cook (it's cheaper and more environmentally friendly), but if you buy them canned, you get the bonus ingredient of the water from the can of beans, now known by a cooler alias: "aquafaba." Aquafaba can be used to replace egg whites, and it can be transformed into a delicious homemade mayo (see "Make It/Buy It," p. 21).

Coconut Milk (Canned)

Keep a full-fat can of coconut milk in your refrigerator at all times so you can have fresh whipped cream on demand. Keep a few cans in the pantry for a curry or to add creamy richness to soups and stews (see the Red Curry recipe, p. 118.). It's also a common ingredient in vegan desserts.

Dried Mushrooms

Fresh mushrooms don't have a terribly long shelf life when you bring them home from the market, but dried, they will last all winter. Rehydrate them in boiling water and add to pastas and stews for richness and chewy texture. Use the soaking water as the base of a brown gravy (see the Polenta with Mushroom Sauce recipe, p. 108).

Ground Flaxseed (Flaxseed Meal)

This is the easiest egg replacement for baking or if you need a binder in a burger or meatless ball. Combined with water, it will develop the thick, somewhat slimy texture of a whisked egg. It's also very high in protein and can be added to smoothies and soups without anyone really noticing.

Heart of Palm

Another salad bar ingredient that is now recognized as a versatile meat substitute, often for seafood dishes. Canned heart of palm has a soft, stringy texture and can be flattened, breaded, and fried like walleye, or shredded to create a mock crab cake. It can even be pulverized in the blender to create a light, lemony cream sauce (see the Summer Pasta with Creamy Sauce recipe, p. 120).

Jackfruit

If you've got a lot of time on your hands and are unfamiliar with the jackfruit, go to your local Asian market and buy one. Then spend many hours on YouTube learning how to attack this terrifying beast. Or look for canned versions, now becoming more widely available in grocery stores. Similar to heart of palm, jackfruit has a meaty, stringy texture, but you'll want to be sure to sauté it first before dumping your favorite barbecue sauce on it for a mock pulled pork sandwich.

Lentils

Lentils make a great substitute in recipes that call for ground meat (see the Cincinnati Chili recipe, p. 96). They are cheap and fast-cooking, and they maintain a firm texture in burgers and stews.

Liquid Smoke, Smoked Paprika, Smoked Salt

These are three ingredients to use to replicate the smoky flavor of bacon or ham. Vegetables sautéed with smoked paprika result in beautiful color and depth. Chilis or stews benefit from a few dashes of liquid smoke. And smoked salt sprinkled on popcorn is the best.

Miso

Usually you find it refrigerated, but it's also available as a shelf-stable item, so it's making this list. It stores well in the freezer once opened. A salty, umami ingredient, it can be added to soups, stews, and sauces of all types. On a cold day, or if you're feeling a little under the weather, a scoop of miso added to boiling water with a generous squirt of sriracha works wonders. Add tofu, noodles, dried mushrooms, and green onions (if you can manage making it to the store).

Nutritional Yeast

It looks like fish food and has a cringeworthy nickname ("nooch"), but this dried, deactivated yeast is very versatile. It gives a nutty, cheesy flavor to creamy sauces (see the Mac and Cheese recipe, p. 84) and is a great popcorn topper. Roughly pulse it with some toasted nuts, salt, pepper, and garlic powder to use as a Parmesan-replacing topping for pasta (see the Summer Pasta with Creamy Sauce recipe, p. 120).

Oats

Oats for breakfast of course, but also . . . Oats can be blended with water and transformed into milk. Oats can be mixed with peanut butter for homemade protein bars. Oats can be pulverized into gluten-free flour. Oats can bulk up veggie burgers and thicken a creamy vegetable bisque. It's a good thing they're cheap, because once you start using them for all these things, they'll go fast.

Raw Cashews

Soaked in boiling water and blended, raw cashews provide a thick, creamy base for desserts and vegan "dairy" products. They have a natural sweetness, so if you're going to use them in a savory manner, add apple cider vinegar, salt, and maybe some garlic to balance it out.

Soy Curls

Mock meats can be mysterious (see "What's in This Stuff?", p. 26), but Butlers Soy Curls are a simple, classic, pantry-friendly option with one ingredient—whole soybeans. It's up to you to flavor them. If your local bulk store doesn't carry them, their website sells direct and has a recipe section. They are a perfect substitute for shredded chicken in flavorful sauce-based dishes (see the Hungarian Paprikash recipe, p. 125) and are easily transformed into jerky.

Spices

Plant-based recipes rely heavily on spices, so you may find yourself going through those little bottles from the baking aisle really quickly. When you're ready to buy replacements, buy spices in glass bottles so that when they're empty, you can buy spices in bulk and refill them. A favorite RBVK resource for spices is Milwaukee-based Penzey's Spices. Known for their liberal politics and adorable squat glass jars, their website sells bagged spices directly and features a wide selection of vegan recipes.

Sun-Dried Tomatoes

Like dried mushrooms, it's nice to have a bag of these on hand to rehydrate for a rich pasta dish or to add to a hummus or dip.

Tomato Paste

Buy the paste in a tube or glass jar so you can use a little at a time without wasting what remains when you open a whole can. A scoop of tomato paste in cooked greens is a secret of vegan soul food enthusiasts. A scoop in a homemade vegetable burger or meatless ball helps it bind, along with adding umami flavor and moisture.

Vital Wheat Gluten

With a name almost as unappetizing as its pantry friend, nutritional yeast, vital wheat gluten is the main ingredient in seitan, a meat alternative that's been around for centuries. (The first documentation of it being used dates to China in the sixth century!) Simply put, it's flour that's had the starch washed out of it, leaving only the stretchy, chewy gluten part behind. You can find it in most grocery stores in the Bob's Red Mill section. Mixing it with water and spices allows you to create a sticky dough that can be formed into shapes, that can then be steamed or boiled, then browned. Many store-bought mock meats have wheat gluten as a main ingredient, but learning to make your own allows you to adjust the flavors and take out any other mystery ingredients. It's also a fun kitchen science experiment!

Vegetable Bouillon Cubes

In a perfect world, we'd save our scraps and make broth to have a surplus always on hand. If you have time for that, that's fantastic! But as an alternative to buying carton after carton of liquid broth, try out a few different brands of little bouillon cubes to see which ones you like. Always keep some in your pantry for a soup or gravy.

Walnuts

While cashews seem to be more versatile when raw, toasted walnuts offer better texture and flavor. Chopped, they can be added to a pasta sauce in place of ground meat. Mixed with chopped sautéed mushrooms, vegetables, and a grain, they make a great filling for stuffed cabbage, lasagna, or stuffed shells. Ground and cooked with brown sugar, they become the most wonderful pastry filling (see the Kolache recipe, p. 164).

MACHINERY

While the items below are certainly not required for these recipes, the following kitchen equipment (referred to here as "machinery" because this is the Rust Belt Vegan Kitchen after all) may make your life a little easier and save you some prep time.

Air Fryer

Not just for healthy french fries, an air fryer does the best job of getting tofu crispy on all sides without any oil at all. When you're sautéing or frying tofu in a pan, the fragile tofu can break when you flip it to brown all sides. The air fryer solves that problem by evenly cooking it on all sides at once. Most air fryers also have a dehydrate setting, so try it for making tofu jerky (see "Make It/Buy It," p. 25), crispy chickpeas (see the garnish for the Roasted Squash soup, p. 57), or for dehydrating mushrooms before they expire.

> *Quick Crispy Tofu:* Press and cube a block of firm tofu. Let it sit in your favorite marinade for 10 minutes or so. Toss with a tablespoon of cornstarch. Heat the air fryer to 400°F and cook for 10 minutes. Shake the basket once or twice during cooking.

Immersion Blender

An immersion blender is a space-saving tool that is perfect for making homemade vegan mayo. If you're looking to purchase one, upgrade to one that also has a whisk attachment (for fresh coconut whipped cream) and a small food processor/chopper attachment (to make a quick batch of faux Parmesan from walnuts, see p. 121). It's also great for pureeing a sauce or bisque while it's still in its pot on the stove, avoiding the dangerous task of transferring hot liquids to your blender.

Rice Cooker

Rice cookers are a staple appliance in many kitchens, but a lot of midwesterners have grown up on instant rice and have never really learned to cook rice properly. Save yourself the trouble of mastering the art of perfect rice and get a rice cooker. It can also be used to quickly cook lentils and quinoa, and it requires no attention once you start it up.

Tofu Press

Pressing tofu can be messy. Is it necessary? For the best texture in many dishes, it is. Do you really need a little plastic appliance that helps you do it? It depends on how often you're eating tofu. If you make it often for frozen breakfast sandwiches or stir-frys, and you're sick of soggy towels and tofu water dripping off your countertops from pressing the curd between cutting boards, a tofu press is a pretty nice little device to have. TofuBud makes a press the exact size of a standard block of tofu, and it contains the water and presses it all out in about 15 minutes.

Vitamix

You'll see references to "high-powered blenders" in many recipes, but most experienced cooks know this means a Vitamix. The company was founded in 1921 with various tools to help people eat more healthy foods, but Vitamix became known for blending in the late 1930s. The family felt then, as they do today, that blending whole foods can transform the healthy kitchen. The Barnard's built their legacy around whole food health, with fourth-generation family member Jodi Berg, PhD, leading the company as President and CEO. This commitment and product performance makes it a favorite investment of the RBVK. A Vitamix will turn cashews into rich cream, pulverize grains into homemade flours, and blend hot soup right in the blending container.

> **Homemade Peanut Butter:** Combine 5 cups roasted peanuts, 1 cup peanut oil, 1 cup brown sugar, and 1 teaspoon kosher salt in a Vitamix and blend until smooth and well incorporated. Stop and scrape down the sides of the container a few times. —*Matt Fish, owner of Melt Bar and Grilled, Cleveland, OH*

Vegetti

You splurged on a Vitamix, now save yourself some money by passing over that expensive electric spiralizer. Instead, head to the As Seen on TV aisle at your corner pharmacy and get yourself a Vegetti. The simple handheld one is all you need. Turns carrots and zucchinis into pretty spirals in minutes, and you get a bicep workout to boot.

Quick Raw Zucchini Salad: Spiralize two zucchinis and a carrot. Toss into a colander with a a few pinches of salt and let sit a minute. Squeeze out the excess water. Drizzle with olive oil, a big squeeze of lemon juice, a dash of red pepper flakes, and half a handful of sunflower seeds.

MAKE IT/BUY IT

Plant-based alternatives to dairy and meat products are more widely available now than ever before. Supporting small companies (like the midwestern companies featured in this book!) that are working to make these products more available (and delicious) feels good. But if you have a little time on your hands, making up a batch of a homemade version can be satisfying. You do you.

Mayo

Up until recently, egg-free, plant-based mayo was only found in health food stores. Follow Your Heart launched its Vegenaise product in 1977 with little competition. But now you can find vegan mayo at mainstream stores—Target has one in its Good & Gather line, and even Hellman's has launched a egg-free version.

Store-bought is convenient, but to save money and customize the ingredients to your taste, you may want to make your own from a few simple ingredients. The RBVK has tested multiple recipes, but by far our favorite is based on aquafaba, the water found in a can of chickpeas. You can then mash up the chickpeas and mix with the mayo, celery, and red onion for a batch of mock tuna salad. No waste!

Aquafaba Mayo: In a large mason jar, pour in 1/2 cup aquafaba. Blend with an immersion blender until light and fluffy. Slowly add 2 cups of canola oil. The mixture will thicken and start to look like mayo. Start seasoning with 1/2 teaspoon of salt, 3 teaspoons of red or white vinegar, and 2 teaspoons of maple syrup or another liquid sweetener. Taste and adjust the flavors. You can add a teaspoon of mustard, garlic or onion powder, or sriracha if you want a spicy mayo. Don't worry if it's a bit thin at first, it will thicken up a bit when refrigerated.

Eggs

There are all sorts of ways to replace eggs in recipes. Some vegan baking recipes simply substitute eggs with a mashed banana. If you're looking for a flavorless option, Bob's Red Mill Egg Replacer is a classic product made from simple ingredients:

tapioca flour, potato starch, baking soda, and psyllium husk. It's great to have a bag on hand for baked goods and savory batters. (The back label tells you exactly how to use it.) For even fewer ingredients, just mix water with flax meal. It will add a bit of a nutty flavor. (Find it in the baking aisle. Aldi carries an affordable house brand.)

> **Flax Egg**: For the equivalent of one egg, whisk 1 tablespoon of flax meal with 3 tablespoons of warm water. Let rest a few minutes, then add to your recipe.

But what about that omelet? A mashed banana is not going to cut it! One of the newest products in the egg substitute market is JUST Egg. It looks like mustard—even the container does—and is found in the dairy section (I spotted it at Target recently). It squirts out into a frying pan with the same look as an already-scrambled-to-perfection egg, and it firms up in a very similar way. There are lots of recipes online for vegan omelets and quiches—some using blended silken tofu, some using chickpea flour—but the JUST Egg scientists have spent years mastering their mung bean miracle product, so this may be something you want to try.

Milk

Plant-based milks are everywhere now. Even Dunkin' Donuts has more than one nondairy option. Try almond, oat, and the various nut ones to see what you like. Watch the sugar and added ingredients, though, as they will vary. While the refrigerated milks tend to taste better plain, it's nice to have a shelf-stable carton or two in the pantry (one unsweetened, one sweetened) for recipes.

In a pinch, you can make one yourself. One thing to note is that because it'll have no preservatives, you'll have to consume the milk within a few days. And while you don't need special equipment (just a blender will do), you do need a good strainer and a piece of cheesecloth to keep the milk from being grainy. Or use "a clean T-shirt," say the very resourceful chefs at Minimalist Baker (minimalistbaker.com), who have lots more tips for making plant-based milks.

Here are some basic ratios. For any of these, adjust the amount of water depending on your desired thickness, and add a liquid sweetener, pinch of salt, and vanilla extract if desired.

Oat Milk: Blend 1 cup raw oats and 4 cups water. Strain.

Nut Milk (Raw Almonds or Cashews): Soak 1 cup of nuts overnight. Drain and rinse. Blend with 5 cups water. Strain.

Rice Milk: Soak 3/4 cup of uncooked white rice in hot water for two hours. Drain and rinse. Blend with 4 cups water. Strain.

Whipped Cream

Reddi-wip makes a dairy-free coconut whipped topping that sits right next to its classic product in mainstream groceries. A similar product was spotted at Aldi recently, but, like many Aldi products, may never be seen again. While you won't get the fun of the direct can-to-mouth spray, you can make a fresh version at home with two ingredients, and you can control the amount of sugar.

Coconut Whipped Cream: Chill a can of full-fat coconut milk in the fridge overnight. When you open the can, the solids will have risen to the top and separated from the liquid. Scoop the solid part into a bowl and beat with a mixer until peaks form. (If it seems too thick, add a small bit of the water from the can.) Add powdered sugar to taste. Returning to the refrigerator to chill again before serving will firm it back up a bit more.

Cheese/Sour Cream/Cream Cheese

Tofutti has been the classic brand for nondairy products since the 1980s. Founder David Mintz started creating these products for his catering clients that kept kosher. But while Tofutti remains a consumer favorite, it now shares the cooler case with other popular brands such as Miyokos, Kite Hill, and Violife (ranked #1 on *Good Housekeeping*'s 2021 list).

There are also smaller and more local boutique brands (see our recipe submission from Cincinnati-based Mad Cheese founder on p. 92), so do some sampling to see what you like.

 RBVK Tip: Look for an ingredient like tapioca flour if you're looking for your cheese to melt and stretch.

While firm, sliceable cheeses are a little more difficult to make at home, softer cheese dips and spreads are a breeze. The sauce for the Mac and Cheese (p. 84) makes a fantastic queso base that had meat eaters swooning in the RBVK test kitchen. Soaked cashews with salt and a splash of vinegar replicate the creaminess sour cream adds to paprikash (see Hungarian Paprikash, p. 125).

Here's a simple tofu-based spread to try on bagels. You will taste the flavor of the tofu a bit, so if that's a turnoff, adjust the seasonings. For a savory version, add diced vegetables, herbs, or spices. For a sweet version, skip the garlic and onion powder, and instead add a little more sweetener and a scoop of strawberry jam.

Tofu Cream Cheese: Strain a 14 oz. package of extra firm tofu. Squeeze out as much water as you can by pressing it with the back of a wooden spoon in your strainer. Put the tofu in a blender or food processor and add 1 tablespoon of lemon juice, 1 teaspoon of salt, 1/4 teaspoon garlic powder, 1/4 teaspoon onion powder, 1 tablespoon of sweetener, and 3 tablespoons of vegan butter. Blend and adjust to taste. Add a splash of plant milk if it's too thick, but it will thicken a bit more in the refrigerator.

 RBVK Tip: Looking for a replacement for Parmesan? Check out the walnut topping to the Summer Creamy Pasta (p. 120).

Hot Dogs

In the ancient days of the RBVK, when craving an old-fashioned hot dog, one needed to drive to the local health food store to find a dusty can of Loma Linda Big Franks. While that same Loma Linda brand is still available online, there are brands aplenty in grocery stores now. So many so that we purchased a variety for a group of meat-eaters and nonmeat eaters to test at a traditional Sunday weenie roast. The nonmeat eaters tended to prefer the Field Roast brand dogs, which come in a variety of flavors such as Smoked Apple Sage and Italian Garlic and Fennel and are more "sausage" than "hot dog." The meateaters commented that brands like Smart Life and Morning Star were closer to the homogenous, salty dogs you'd get at the stadium on Dollar Dog Night.

You can make your own hot dogs using vital wheat gluten (seitan), but the process is a bit tedious. You have to make the dough, then shape and wrap each dog individually in foil and steam them to hold their shape before grilling. The thinner shape of a hot dog is more difficult to recreate and maintain than that of a burger patty. If you have the time, it's an interesting kitchen experiment to attempt. You can use familiar spices from your traditional family sausage recipes, but next time, you'll most likely go back to the store-bought kind.

 RBVK Tip: When grilling, always oil your weenies! The lack of fat in most plant-based dogs (whether homemade or store-bought) lends them to drying out on the grill. Brushing them with oil first gets the outside crispy and gives you those desirable grill lines.

Jerky

The RBVK loves a salty, chewy, protein-packed jerky, and our favorite store-bought version is Louisville Vegan Jerky. It was launched in 2012 when founder Stanley Chase mistakenly overcooked a meatless barbecue dish. You can buy it directly from their online store, or find it at Whole Foods or possibly your local market (their site has a store finder too).

All kinds of recipes can be found online, using everything from mushrooms, to eggplant to watermelon! Marinating and oven-baking Butlers Soy Curls (see "Pantry Staples," p. 13) is a quick and popular option, but for the best taste and texture, we love the classic recipe from 2002's *How it All Vegan* (by Tanya Barnard and Sarah Kramer, Arsenal Pulp Press) that involves marinating sliced tofu overnight and then baking it at a low temp for several hours. You can't find the exact recipe online, so go ahead and buy the book—because aren't printed cookbooks so much better than trying to read recipes off your phone?

WHAT'S IN THIS STUFF?

People often ask about the decision to use "fake meat" in vegan dishes. There seem to be two different camps on this one. We include recipes in this book that speak to both.

#1. Fake Meat That Is Nothing Like Meat

Consider the "carrot dog." Yes, vegetarians have been known to marinate and steam a full carrot and put it on a hot dog bun. This was a popular enough idea that Bolthouse Farms (the company that makes the popular bottled juices and smoothies) recently launched their own ready-to-go version in a shrink-wrapped eight-pack that looks similar to a pack of beef hot dogs. Carrot dogs are meant to be eaten *like* a hot dog, but they're not fooling anyone. The marinade may have a nice salty flavor that works well with a soft bun and all the fixings, but it in no way looks or tastes like meat. Also consider the wide variety of veggie burgers. The early versions at health food cafés in the 1980s were clearly made of chopped carrots and broccoli, beans, or lentils that were lightly smashed, so you could see exactly what you were eating. These appeal to people who really like vegetables and like to look at them when they eat them. If someone does not eat meat because of a compassion for animals (or because meat simply grosses them out), this is most likely the type they prefer.

#2. Fake Meat That Looks Like Meat

As plant-based culinary technology has evolved, we've been introduced to all kinds of new products that very much replicate the texture and taste of meat. Tofurky and Morning Star were early brands to do this, using vital wheat gluten and soy to get a chewy texture. More recently we've been introduced to Beyond Burgers and Impossible Burgers, which use plant proteins as a base to replicate not just texture and flavor but even the pink-to-brown color change of a beef burger cooking on the grill. This can be spooky to some, but these products are an alternative for people who like meat and may be transitioning away from it because of health or environmental reasons. Ingredients in these products vary. Read the labels and learn what's in them so you have a good answer when someone asks. No matter what you're eating, it's nice to know what it is and where it came from! If you like the meaty look and texture of these brands but aren't sure what the ingredients are, try making some yourself using seitan. Bob's Red Mill vital wheat gluten has directions for basic seitan on the back of the bag, which you can then flavor and shape and cook various ways.

BREAK FAST

BREAKFAST SCRAMBLE

Sarah Hastings
Home Chef
Berea, OH

" This is a quick, simple breakfast that's easy to make. I like to keep it simple with just the green pepper, but you can bulk up the scramble with other vegetables and crumbled vegetarian sausage if you like. I also use this scramble as the filling for a batch of breakfast sandwiches I stock in the freezer. Spoon the scramble onto a vegan English muffin or bagel, add a slice of vegan cheese and hot sauce, wrap them individually and freeze. You can microwave them in the morning when you're in a rush. If you're not in a rush, make this scramble along with my Pumpkin Muffins on the next page, some roasted potatoes, and a big fruit salad for an epic brunch."

Serves 4

INGREDIENTS

14 ounces extra firm tofu

2 tablespoons olive oil

1 green pepper, diced

1 teaspoon salt

1 teaspoon garlic powder

1 teaspoon cumin

1/2 teaspoon chili powder

1/2 teaspoon turmeric

INSTRUCTIONS

Gently wrap the tofu with a kitchen towel and press between two cutting boards or plates, weighting it down with something heavy to press some of the water out. Give it about 5 minutes or so.

Heat the oil in the skillet. Add the green peppers and sauté for about 5 minutes on medium heat. Add the spices and stir for 1 minute.

Crumble the tofu and add it to the pan. Cook until tofu starts to get a little brown (another 5 minutes or so). Add a bit of water if the pan seems dry.

RBVK Tip: For a more egg-like flavor, try using black salt (see "Pantry Staples," p. 13) in place of regular salt. Also, turmeric stains everything! I like to have one wooden spoon designated as a turmeric spoon so that all my wooden utensils don't turn yellow.

PUMPKIN MUFFINS

Sarah Hastings
Home Chef
Berea, OH

" I have been a vegetarian for over two decades, but began eating mostly vegan about twelve years ago due to my son's multitude of allergies. Since then, we have just worked at adapting recipes and dishes to ensure he never feels left out or excluded. We want his food options to match everyone else's."

Makes approximately 1 dozen muffins

INGREDIENTS

1/2 cup canola oil

2 tablespoons ground flax

6 tablespoons hot water

1/2 cup pumpkin (1/2 of a 15-ounce can)

1 cup sugar

1 cup gluten-free flour (I usually use Bob's Red Mill)

1 tablespoon cinnamon

1 1/4 teaspoons baking soda

1/4 teaspoon salt

INSTRUCTIONS

Preheat the oven to 350°F.

Mix the flax and water, occasionally stirring. Let it rest for a few minutes. Do not add to the other ingredients until the flax begins to absorb the water.

Mix sugar, oil, flax mix, and pumpkin by hand until combined.

Add in flour, cinnamon, baking soda, and salt. Mix by hand.

Scoop into lined muffin tin.

Bake for 30 minutes or until a toothpick comes out clean.

CHUNKY SCONES

Oscar Narváez

Professional Chef | The Chunky Scone
Waukegan, Illinois
thechunkyscones.com
Facebook: @thechunkyscones
Instagram: @thechunkyscone

" Scones are very close to my heart because they were one of my first creations when I became vegan. I started my vegan baked goods company in 2015 at a little holiday community market in the neighborhood of Pilsen, in Chicago. I have always had some degree of chunkiness in me, so I named it The Chunky Scone. The first day of the market, I brought two baskets of packaged scones, and to my surprise, all of them sold out! The scones were the key that opened the door to my business, which now creates all kinds of vegan baked goods. They are such an underrated delicacy in the world of baked goods. When people buy and eat my scones, it fills me with joy. This recipe can be completely customized by you. I invite you to get creative with a combination of your favorite ingredients! My personal favorite is chocolate chips with peanut butter. If you want to make a different flavor, omit the chips and peanut butter and add 1/2 cup of your desired ingredients, such as dried fruit or nuts."

Makes 8 scones

INGREDIENTS

2 cups all-purpose flour*

1 tablespoon baking powder

1/4 cup vegetable oil

1/2 teaspoon salt

2 tablespoons sugar

1 cup any plant-based milk

3 tablespoons milled flax seed (optional)

1/2 cup vegan chocolate chips

3 tablespoons of peanut butter

1/4 cup desired garnish (cinnamon or raw sugar)

INSTRUCTIONS

Preheat your oven to 370°F.

In a clean mixing bowl, add your flour, baking powder, salt, sugar, and flax seed. Proceed to mix with a whisk until all ingredients have been evenly distributed.

Add your plant-based milk and vegetable oil. Mix all ingredients with a spatula until you have formed a uniform dough. Feel free to use your hands to mix at this point.

Add your the peanut butter and chocolate chips (or desired flavor ingredients).

Shape the dough into a ball. Put on a plate or a cutting board and flatten the dough with your hand until you have about 1 1/2 to 2 inches of thickness and it is about 8 inches in length or circumference.

Cut your flattened dough 4 times, as if you were making a cross, and then cut it again to look like an 8-pointed star. By then, you should have 8 scones that you can place on a baking tray.

Garnish your scones with any ingredient of your choice. Cinnamon powder makes for a great finisher when it comes to dried fruits, but feel free to use any ingredient you may want. Sugar in the Raw also works great.

Bake for about 25 minutes until golden brown. Let them rest for 15 minutes or so. Enjoy, and keep livin' la vida Chunky!

Chef's Tip: I highly recommend using flours with a protein content of 4 or more grams of protein per 1/4 cup. If a flour of lesser proteins is used, the dough might be too watery.

 RBVK Tip: Our test kitchen used this base recipe and opted for a savory version, adding 1/4 teaspoon of garlic powder, 1/2 cup pitted Kalamata olives, cracked black pepper, and garnishing the scones with smoked salt and dried rosemary.

CHOCOLATE CHERRY GRANOLA

Kelly Wright
Restaurant Owner | Borderline Cafe
Lakewood, OH
borderlinecafe.com
Facebook: @borderlinecafe

If your childhood breakfasts consisted of a steady rotation of Cocoa Puffs, Count Chocula, and Cocoa Krispies, consider this your best option for an adult version. Unlike those store-bought cereals of old, it's packed with protein and bonus flavors for max sophistication.

Makes about 8 servings

INGREDIENTS

3 tablespoons coconut oil

1/3 cup peanut butter

1/3 cup honey

1/2 teaspoon salt

2 teaspoons cinnamon

1 teaspoon almond extract

1 teaspoon coconut extract

3 cups old-fashioned rolled oats

1/2 cup pecans

1/2 cup cocoa almonds

1/2 cup dried cherries

INSTRUCTIONS

Preheat the oven to 325°F.

In a small saucepan, combine the coconut oil, peanut butter, honey, salt, cinnamon, almond extract, and coconut extract.

Simmer until combined.

In a separate mixing bowl, combine the oats and pecans.

Pour peanut butter and honey mixture over the oats and pecans. Stir to fully coat and combine.

Line a baking sheet with parchment paper and spread the oats and pecans to cover the baking sheet.

Bake for 40 minutes, stirring occasionally, until the mixture has browned and crisped.

Cool completely, then mix in the almonds and cherries. Don't worry—the granola will get crispier after it cools.

PALACINKY (SWEET CREPE)

Meredith Pangrace
Home Chef
Cleveland, OH

" I grew up eating my grandma's Slovak food, but the first time I had palacinky was in Prague on a high school trip. I loved the light, delicate pancake with whipped cream and strawberries, and when I came home to rave to my grandma about this dessert (that I couldn't remember the name of), she just rolled her eyes and said, "Oh, that's just palacinky," as if it was just a humble breakfast, not worthy of all my excitement. But from that point on, she would offer to make it for me on morning visits.

Crepes can take a little practice. You don't need a special pan—a regular frying pan will do. Your crepes will be the size of the diameter of the pan. You want a thin layer of batter to cover the whole bottom. I still always overcook the first one, so don't worry if it takes a couple tries to get the nice golden color you're looking for. If you don't have fresh strawberries, use your favorite jam."

Serves two, makes about 4 crepes, depending on size of pan

INGREDIENTS

Batter:

1 1/2 cups all-purpose flour

1 tablespoon cornstarch

1 tablespoon sugar

1 teaspoon vanilla extract

1/4 teaspoon salt

2 tablespoons vegetable oil

2 cups plant milk, vanilla flavored works well

For filling:

1 pint strawberries

1 tablespoon sugar

Vegan butter for frying pan

Powdered sugar for sprinkling on top

Bonus Toppings:
Chocolate Syrup
Sliced bananas
Lemon wedge
Coconut whipped cream (see "Make It/Buy It" p. 21)

INSTRUCTIONS

Toss the strawberries in the sugar and set aside.

In a blender, mix all the batter ingredients.

Over medium heat, melt enough butter in your pan to cover the bottom.

Slowly ladle in enough batter to coat the bottom. Tilt the pan right away to cover the whole surface. As you get more experienced with the batter, you can aim for a thinner coat for the most delicate crepe, but do try and make it thinner than a pancake to start.

Cook until the top bubbles and looks dry. Carefully lift an edge with your spatula to check that the bottom is golden.

Gently flip and cook for about another minute. Remove from the pan when both sides are golden.

Repeat with the remaining batter to make multiple crepes. The amount you make will depend on the size of your pan.

To serve, scoop some strawberries into the center of the crepe and roll, somewhat tightly. Top with powdered sugar and whatever other add-ons you like.

ZUCCHINI MUFFINS

Dave Huffman
Professional Chef| | Bitchy Vegan Homo
Cleveland, OH
bvhbakery.com
Instagram: @bitchyveganhomo

"I'm about as Rust Belt as you can get—it just doesn't feel like home for me if there isn't a steel mill a few miles away. I've always loved to cook, and my borderline sugar addiction led me to create my own vegan baked goods. One night while I was cooking dinner, a guest teased, 'Shut up you Bitchy Vegan Homo!' I immediately claimed the name as my business.

Growing up in Pittsburgh, one of my favorite foods was my Aunt Helen's zucchini bread. Made from the abundance of zucchini in my grandmother's garden, Aunt Helen's zucchini bread was incredibly moist and perfectly spiced. My muffins are a great tribute to my aunt's original. They are a wonderful breakfast food or a perfect sweet treat any time of day."

Makes 8 muffins

INGREDIENTS

10 ounces flour (about 2 cups)

1 tablespoon baking powder

1 teaspoon cinnamon

1/2 teaspoon ground ginger

1/2 teaspoon baking soda

1/2 teaspoon salt

1/8 teaspoon ground cloves

7 ounces brown sugar (about 1 cup)

3/4 cup soy milk

1/3 cup oil

1 teaspoon vanilla

2 tablespoons ground flax seed

6 tablespoons water

1 1/2 cups grated zucchini

INSTRUCTIONS

Preheat the oven to 350° F.

Grease a muffin tin with Pam or vegetable oil.

In a large bowl, combine the flour, baking powder, baking soda, cinnamon, ginger, salt, and cloves and whisk together. Set aside.

In a small bowl, add the water and flaxseed. Stir and set aside to allow the flax to gel up a bit to be used as the egg replacer. Set aside.

In a medium bowl, combine the brown sugar, soy milk, oil, and vanilla. Mix together with a whisk until well combined.

Add the flaxseed mixture and grated zucchini to the wet ingredients and stir to combine.

Add the wet ingredients to the dry and mix until just combined. Do not over mix!

Fill each muffin tin to the top so you'll have a nice "muffin top" when they bake. (Note that this recipe will make 8 muffins, so you'll have some empty spots in your tin. This doesn't mean that you're inadequate. I mean, it also doesn't mean that you aren't inadequate, but that has nothing to do with muffin tin capacity.)

Bake for 23 minutes. Test the muffins with a toothpick to see if they are done. If the toothpick doesn't come out clean, bake for a few more minutes and test again.

Remove the muffins from the tin immediately (and carefully). Cool the muffins completely on a wire rack.

 RBVK Tip: While quick to admit to inadequacies, the RBVK tester was able to get 11 respectable-size muffins from this recipe.

FENUGREEK PANCAKES

Kirti Sheth

Professional Chef | Arya Bhavan Restaurant Vegan
& Gluten Free Indian Cuisine
Chicago, IL
Facebook: @AryaBhavanChicago

I grew up in India around my family's farming and agriculture business, which my family still runs and which shaped my eating habits. I still remember the excitement I would feel as a little girl picking up the fresh fenugreek, smelling it, and anticipating all the tasty and healthy dishes we were going to cook with it. After learning how to cook from my mom, my sisters, and later, my mother-in-law, I finally followed my passion in 1998 when I opened the Arya Bhavan restaurant in Chicago. My greatest source of joy is to hear my customers say they feel better when they eat my food. I continue to experiment with new recipes and twists on traditional recipes, and I am working on a cookbook of my own vegan, gluten-free Indian/Indian fusion recipes. It will be available to order at aryabhavan.com

You can eat these pancakes warm or cold. Good for breakfast, brunch, lunch, or dinner. They can last two days in the refrigerator once made. Look for fresh fenugreek (aka methi leaves) in international market stores or Indian/Chinese stores. You can also grow fenugreek in a pot at home, indoors or outdoors."

Serves 4

Ingredients

1 large bunch of fenugreek leaves; chop into small pieces, removing the stem, and wash 4–5 times to remove all the dirt.
1/2 cup Cream of Wheat
2 cups chickpea flour
1/2 cup sorghum flour
1/4 cup rice flour
1 cup wheat flour
4 cups water

1 tablespoon salt

1 tablespoon turmeric powder

A handful of washed, chopped cilantro

5 cloves garlic

4 pieces Thai chili

1 inch fresh ginger

1/2 red onion, finely chopped

1/2 tomato, finely chopped

1 very ripe banana, mashed

Olive oil

INSTRUCTIONS

Add all the ingredients except for the onion, tomato, and banana to a bowl and whisk very well.

Add the onion, tomato, and mashed banana and whisk.

The batter should be rather thick. Let it sit for 10 minutes.

Take a nonstick frying pan or skillet, greased with a little olive oil, and heat it quickly to medium heat.

Spoon 2 ladles (or 1, for a smaller pancake) of batter into the skillet. Flatten it with the back of the ladle to give it a round pancake shape.

Turn the flame to low. After 1–2 minutes, flip the pancake onto the other side and cook for another minute. Flip once more on each side (1 minute for each side). Cooking time should be about 5 minutes per pancake. Both sides should be golden brown.

Repeat until you use all the batter. You might have to spray a little olive oil on the pan again after each couple of pancakes. Eat with a pickle or ketchup.

Chef's Notes: For spicier taste, use 8 cloves of garlic, 8 pieces of Thai chili, and 1 1/4 inch of fresh ginger).

To make this recipe gluten free, do not add the Cream of Wheat or wheat flour, and only use 3 cups of water.

The tomato, onion, and banana can be mixed and used as a topping for the pancakes.

 RBVK Tip: Our test kitchen says, "Pancakes, pickles, and ketchup!? Genius!"

BLUEBERRY LEMON MUFFINS

Robert Mar
Professional Chef | The Vegan Comfort Kitchen
Cleveland, OH
thevegancomfortkitchen.com

"I've been a professional chef for almost thirty years. During the pandemic, my girlfriend, Morgan, and I thought it would be fun to start a vegan side business. Like any good chef, I enjoy learning new techniques and different ways to cook. I had to be creative, research, and most importantly, make good tasting food. We think we've done that. We both knew that the vegan community was underserved in variety, price, and quality. We have regular local customers, a nice wholesale account, and a viable thriving shipping business. We have shipped our vegan treats across the nation. It's been fun and has opened a new future for us to consider.

This is a very simple, easy recipe to follow and the muffins always come out great."

Makes 12 standard or 6 jumbo muffins

INGREDIENTS

2 cups all-purpose flour

1 1/4 teaspoons baking powder

1/2 cup granulated sugar

1/2 teaspoon salt

3/4 cup oat milk

1/4 cup avocado oil

2 teaspoons vanilla

1 teaspoon lemon zest

1/2 cup carbonated water (seltzer, club soda, even a citrus soda works)

1 cup blueberries

1/4 teaspoon per muffin of coarse sugar (for topping)

INSTRUCTIONS

Preheat the oven to 350°F.

Combine the wet ingredients in a mixing bowl.

In a separate bowl, combine the dry ingredients.

Add the wet to dry ingredients and mix well.

Fold in berries.

Scoop or spoon out evenly between paper-lined muffin cups.

Top each muffin with 1/4 teaspoon of coarse sugar.

Bake for 32 minutes for standard muffins, or 38 minutes for jumbo.

SOUPS & STEWS

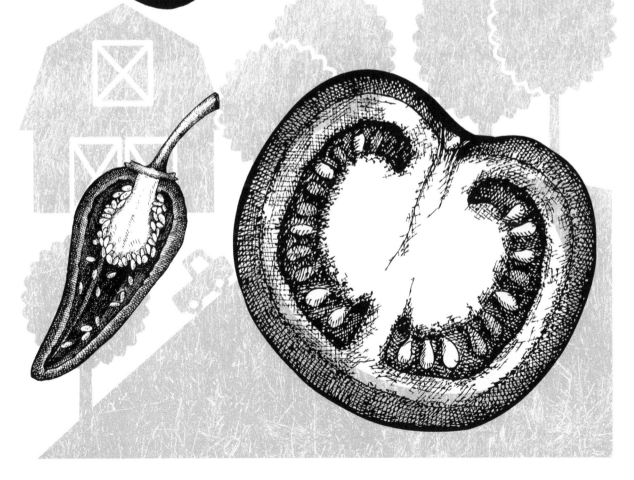

GRANDMA'S MOUNTAIN STEW

Dana Textoris
Home Chef
Lakewood, OH

" I believe that this Mountain Stew gave my family twenty extra years with my grandfather. After a lifetime of Slovenian-style eating, my grandfather had his first open-heart surgery on my first birthday. The doctors at the Cleveland Clinic had the wisdom, even in the eighties, to encourage my grandmother to change his diet to include much less meat, less oil, and lots of vegetables. As a result, I grew up learning to love tofu, lentils, and vegetable-based meals. There would always be a new vegetarian cookbook checked out from the Parma Heights Library on my grandmother's kitchen table so that she could test the recipes before committing to buy the book for her collection. This stew became one of our family's favorites. I'm grateful to my grandmother and her cooking for the gift of so many years I got to have with my grandpa."

Serves 4-6

Ingredients

1 cup cooked kidney beans

2 tablespoons olive oil

1 large onion, chopped

4 cloves garlic, chopped

1 green bell pepper, seeded and chopped coarsely

1 cup green cabbage, chopped coarsely

1/2 cup diced russet potatoes

1 can (16 ounces) tomatoes with liquid

1 tablespoon chili powder (or more to taste)

1/2 teaspoon ground cumin

1/3 cup uncooked brown rice

4 cups water or vegetable broth

Salt and pepper to taste

INSTRUCTIONS

In a large pot over medium-high heat, heat oil and cook onion and garlic, stirring, until onion is soft (3–5 minutes).

Add vegetables, tomatoes, and spices. Cook, stirring, for 3 minutes.

Add rice, water or broth, and beans. Cover and cook over low heat until stew is thick, and beans and rice are tender, up to 2 hours (or sooner if it reaches your desired consistency).

Season with salt and pepper.

ITALIAN WEDDING SOUP

Holly Pangrace
Home Chef
Akron, OH

"   As a child, I had a deep association with my Italian heritage. We held all of the traditions one would expect: sauce on Sunday, homemade treats associated with various saints' days, trips to DeVitis Italian specialty store in Akron for salty provolone, meats, and olives. My great-grandmother was our matriarch. I feel so lucky that I got to experience her willingness to give us everything she had, even though she herself had very little.

    After my first daughter was born, my mother came to stay with us, and every day at lunchtime, she would bring me a big bowl of homemade Italian wedding soup. I chose this recipe because it is symbolic of the love and care of not just my mother, but of the feeling of being loved by the women in my family, rooted in those early days of my childhood."

Serves 6–8

INGREDIENTS

1 tablespoon olive oil

I bag plant-based meatballs (I like the Whole Foods brand, but any kind will do)

1 1/4 cups carrots, diced

1 1/4 cups yellow onion, diced

3/4 cup celery, diced

1 tablespoon garlic, minced

8 cups vegetable stock

2 teaspoons Italian seasoning

Salt and pepper to taste

3/4 cup dry Acini di Pepe pasta

8 ounces fresh spinach

Fresh parsley, roughly chopped, for garnish

Faux Parmesan cheese, for garnish

INSTRUCTIONS

Heat the olive oil in a large soup pot over medium-high heat.

Brown the meatballs in batches for 2–3 minutes.

Remove the meatballs and set aside.

Add the onions, carrots, and celery and sauté for 5 minutes, until softened.

Add the garlic and sauté for 1 minute.

Add the vegetable broth, Italian seasoning, and season with salt and pepper if desired.

Bring to a boil.

Reduce the heat to medium. Add the meatballs and pasta.

Simmer for 10 minutes, until the meatballs are cooked through.

Stir in the spinach.

Garnish with fresh parsley and faux Parmesan.

MATZO BALL SOUP

Linda Zolten Wood
Home Chef
Cleveland, OH

"   I'm from a Jewish background, and I found myself yearning for this comfort food when I became vegan. There are a few important steps in getting the matzo just right, so plan ahead to make the dough in the morning so it can chill all day before you form it into balls and add it to the soup. Also, my recipe calls for a mix of three variations on the vegan egg replacer. (I've tried this recipe with only aquafaba or powdered egg replacement, but the balls fell apart.) Some people take out all of the veggies and leave just a clear broth, but I like the soft vegetables in the soup. I sometimes add broccoli florets or leeks, as long as they're simmered for at least an hour. That way they don't distract from the matzo balls as the star of the show."

Serves 6–8

INGREDIENTS

Matzo balls:

2 matzo meal mix boxes

2 aquafaba egg: 6 tablespoons aquafaba

1 chia egg: dissolve 1 tablespoon chia seeds + 2 1/2 tablespoons warm water

1 flax egg: dissolve 1 tablespoon flax seeds and 3 tablespoons of warm water

Broth:

6 cups water

1 tablespoon of Better than Bouillon Vegetarian No Chicken Base

1 large carrot, chopped in discs

2 stalks celery, chopped medium

1 sweet medium-sized onion, diced

1–3 whole peeled garlic cloves, to taste

Salt to taste

INSTRUCTIONS

Mix your three egg replacers together. Let sit for a few minutes.

Mix the egg replacers into the matzo mix and chill for a whole day.

Bring the water to a boil in a large pot.

Add the bouillon and vegetables and simmer until vegetables are tender.

Roll the matzo dough into small golf-ball-sized balls.

Gently place the balls into the broth, cover, and let simmer for at least another 20 minutes.

SLOVENIAN SAUERKRAUT SOUP (JOTA)

Joe Valencic
Home Chef
Cleveland, OH

" Many recipes from Slovenia reflect the country's position as a cultural crossroads between the Mediterranean, Alpine, and Balkan worlds. This hearty soup blends sauerkraut and smoky paprika with tomato sauce and cannellini beans. It is especially popular in the coastal region of Slovenia along the border with Italy. The longer the soup cooks, the better it tastes. This recipe is Slovenian comfort food for me."

Serves 8

INGREDIENTS

1 pound dried cannellini or kidney beans

1 pound sauerkraut

1 medium onion, chopped

5 cloves garlic, minced

2 tablespoons tomato sauce (more to taste)

1 pound potatoes, peeled and cubed

4 tablespoons flour

4 cups vegetable broth

2 teaspoons smoked paprika

1 tablespoon oil

1 bay leaf

Salt and pepper to taste

INSTRUCTIONS

Sort the beans (for pebbles or debris), rinse, and soak overnight.

Rinse the beans and place them in a large pot. Cover with water by two inches. Bring to a boil, then turn down and simmer until tender, 1–2 hours (depends on the age of the beans), and drain.

In a separate pot, cover potatoes with cold water and bring to a boil. Cook until tender, 10–15 minutes, and drain.

Drain and rinse the sauerkraut, place in a separate saucepan, cover with water, and heat.

In a large pot, sauté onion in oil until golden over medium heat. Stir in flour and a tablespoon of water to make a roux (for thickening). Cook and stir until light brown.

Put the cooked beans, cooked potatoes, cooked sauerkraut, and vegetable broth into the pot with the roux. Add the garlic, bay leaf, tomato sauce, paprika, salt, and pepper. (Optional: mash the beans and potatoes together before adding to saucepan.)

Bring soup to boil, reduce heat, and simmer for 2 hours or more.

Remove bay leaf before serving. For a thinner soup, add any remaining cooking water to taste.

ROASTED SQUASH SOUP WITH CRISPY CHICKPEAS

Jodi Berg
CEO | Vitamix
North Olmsted, OH
Recipe by the Vitamix culinary team

" My grandparents became vegetarians in the 1930s and raised their children that way. My father strayed from a vegetarian lifestyle for many years after leaving home but eventually adopted a non processed, vegan diet that he has not swayed from since.

For those in the Midwest who might have grown up on that kind of diet, our Vitamix team wants to meet people where they are in their health journey, without overwhelming them. We start with showing our customers how easy it is to incorporate whole foods into their diet. We also find tremendous value in a community of people who are on the same journey and therefore deeply appreciate the efforts of the vegan community to unite, educate, and inspire others.

Enjoy the warm flavors of fall with this hearty squash soup, topped with crunchy chickpeas and fresh herbs. The crunchy chickpeas also make a great salad topper or salty snack on their own."

Serves 4-6

ROASTED SQUASH SOUP

INGREDIENTS

2/3 of a large butternut squash, peeled, cut into large chunks

2/3 of a medium yellow onion, peeled, cut into large chunks

2 cloves garlic, peeled

2/3 tablespoon ground cumin

2/3 tablespoon ground turmeric

1/2 cup raw cashews

2 3/4 cup vegetable broth

2/3 cup water

Kosher salt to taste

Ground black pepper to taste

INSTRUCTIONS

Preheat your oven to 400°F. Place cut-up butternut squash cubes in a large bowl. Add 2 tablespoons of avocado oil and sprinkle with salt and pepper. Toss to combine and spread onto a baking sheet lined with parchment paper. Place in the preheated oven, roasting for 40 minutes or until browned and fork tender.

Heat one tablespoon of avocado oil in a pan over medium heat. Once hot, add the onions and cook for 2–3 minutes or until soft and translucent, stirring often. Add in the garlic and cook for 1 more minute until fragrant. Add spices and cook for an additional minute.

Place all ingredients (roasted squash, onion mixture, cashews, vegetable broth, and water) in a pot. Submerge a Vitamix immersion blender below the surface of the liquid or as close to the ingredients as possible.

Start the blender at its lowest speed and increase to its highest speed. Move the immersion blender around, including up and down, to blend the ingredients for approximately 1 minute or until desired consistency is achieved.

CRISPY CHICKPEAS

INGREDIENTS

2/3 can chickpeas, rinsed, drained, dried well

11/3 tablespoon extra-virgin olive oil

2/3 tablespoon smoked paprika

Kosher salt to taste

Ground black pepper to taste

INSTRUCTIONS

Preheat your oven to 400°F and make sure you have a rack in the center. Drain and rinse the can of chickpeas. Lay them out on a plate lined with paper towels and gently pat them dry.

Place the chickpeas in a bowl, add the avocado oil, and stir to coat.

Sprinkle with the smoked paprika, salt, and pepper to stir the coat evenly. Pour onto a large baking sheet lined with parchment paper and spread evenly. Place in the oven and roast for 25–30 minutes or until golden brown and crispy.

Ladle soup into soup bowls and top with the crispy chickpeas, and freshly chopped chives or green onions if desired.

SPICY WHITE BEAN GUMBO

Leigh Ann Wise
Home Chef
Akron, OH

" I'm originally from LA—Lower Alabama. My vegan journey has taken me on a path of evolving some of my favorite Southern dishes into hearty plant-based versions. The unique ingredient in gumbo is filé ('fee-lay'), which is ground leaves from the sassafras tree. If you opt out of including the mock sausage, no worries! There's plenty of flavor going on here. Gumbo simply means "okra," so this recipe is incredibly versatile. Every component can be increased or decreased to taste . . . just make sure you don't skip the okra!"

Serves 6–8

INGREDIENTS

2 cans white beans, drained

1 large onion, diced

6 garlic cloves, minced

4 celery stalks, chopped

1 jalapeno (or other hot pepper of choice), finely diced

1 cup chopped collards (feel free to use more)

1 (12-ounce) bag of frozen okra

2 Beyond Meat Spicy Sausages, chopped (optional)

4 cups vegetable broth

1/4 cup olive oil or vegan butter

4 tablespoons flour (use gluten-free flour if desired)

1 teaspoon salt

1 tablespoon smoked paprika

1 tablespoon fennel seeds

1–2 tablespoons coriander

1 tablespoon cumin

1–2 tablespoons Tony Chachere's Creole Seasoning

1 tablespoon thyme
1/2 teaspoon gumbo filé

Rice (optional):
1 cup basmati rice
1/2 teaspoon salt
4 cups of water

INSTRUCTIONS

Make a roux (pronounced "rue," a French recipe starter that helps thicken a sauce). Heat the oil or butter (I use half oil and half butter) over low to medium heat and slowly add the flour. Stir constantly until it thickens and browns to a rich caramel color or even slightly darker, anywhere from 10–20 minutes. Roux die-hards will even cook it longer . . . low and slow . . . just don't burn it.

Add onion, garlic, celery, jalapeno, and seasoning. Cook until the vegetables begin to soften a little, then gently stir in the beans (and vegan sausage, if using). Cook 5 minutes more.

Slowly add the broth, then the okra and collard greens.

Bring to a boil, then cover it and lower the heat and simmer for 30 minutes or until the beans are very soft. Add more water or broth if needed and adjust the seasoning.

When the beans are soft, turn off heat. Stir in thyme and gumbo filé.

Serve the gumbo as it is or over rice. Try using the rice-cooking technique here.

RICE

Place one cup of basmati rice and 1/2 teaspoon salt into a saucepan and cover with 4 cups of water.

Place over high heat. Bring it to a boil while stirring. Once boiling, reduce heat to a low boil and cook 8–10 minutes until the rice is al dente (still very slightly firm).

Using a strainer that fits into the saucepan, drain the rice and give it a quick rinse with water.

Refill the saucepan with 1/2 inch of water, then place the strainer of al dente rice into the saucepan above the water and cover with aluminum foil or a secure-fitting lid. Bring to a low boil and steam the rice for another 8 minutes.

Remove foil or lid, gently toss the rice with a fork to release steam, and leave uncovered to cool for 5 minutes. Serve.

WEST AFRICAN PEANUT STEW

Joel Tishken
Home Chef
Richmond, IN

" I became vegan the moment I began cooking for myself nearly thirty years ago. My initial motivation was entirely motivated by animal rights. Later, I began to appreciate the benefits to the environment and to humankind. As a Unitarian Universalist minister, being vegan is a way for me to live my values and reimagine a new way of being in nonviolent relationship with animals, nature, and one another. In 2015, I was delighted to find that an Earlham College professor was in the process of starting a monthly vegan potluck group. We named the group RIPE for Richmond Indiana Plant Eaters. We've been meeting monthly ever since."

Serves 4

INGREDIENTS

1 (16-ounce) can plain tomato sauce

4 tablespoons creamy peanut butter

Salt and pepper to taste

1 medium onion, diced

1 large or 2 medium green bell peppers, seeded and diced

1 (16-ounce) can diced tomato (preferably petite)

1 diced jalapeno or serrano (depending on desired heat level)

Chef's Note: Customize the stew with vegetables you have on hand, such as: 1 bunch of chopped leafy greens (spinach, mustard greens, or kale), 1 sweet potato (peeled and diced), 1 plantain (peeled and diced), or 1 cup chopped okra.

INSTRUCTIONS

Combine the tomato sauce and peanut butter in a saucepan. Whisk, then simmer until peanut butter melts.

Season with salt and a generous amount of black pepper.

Add some water or additional tomato sauce if too thick.

Add the diced onion and bell pepper, canned tomatoes, and hot pepper and cook for 10-15 minutes.

Add the additional vegetables.

Simmer stew until all the vegetables are soft.

Serve over rice, couscous, fufu, millet, or mashed yams.

ROASTED TOMATO SOUP

Meg Doerr
Home Chef
Cleveland, OH

" This recipe arose from a midwestern tomato bounty. The best thing about it is that it freezes really well, so when you thaw it in February, it tastes like summer all over again. I usually make five or six batches a summer, and eat it weekly year-round. Although it's super delicious, it's not a very calorie-intensive soup, so make sure to have sides to accompany it, or serve as one course in a multicourse meal. You'll need your largest roasting pan to fit all the tomatoes in."

Serves 8

INGREDIENTS

Summer tomatoes: As many as you can get your hands on. At minimum, you will need enough large tomatoes to fill your pan. For my large roasting pan, this is about 24 large tomatoes or 12 enormous tomatoes; you can add smaller tomatoes and cherry tomatoes to fill in gaps.

12 ounces miso broth (or other broth of your choice)

2 ounces soy sauce

A couple tablespoons of good, dark maple syrup

3 ounces olive oil

A pinch or more of red pepper flakes (amount depends on how spicy you like it)

INSTRUCTIONS

Preheat the oven to 500°F. (No joke!)

Core the tomatoes. Do not remove seeds or skin, just core them, but make sure you get all the hard white part out on the larger ones.

Pack the tomatoes into your roasting pan, cored side up. You want them to be pressed together, their sides touching each other and the sides of the pan.

If you have cherry tomatoes, you can wedge them in the spaces between the big tomatoes once you have all the big tomatoes in place.

Mix the broth, soy sauce, maple syrup, olive oil, and red pepper flakes together.

Pour mixture into each of the "holes" in the tomatoes (where the cores were). Pour the rest of the mixture over the top of the tomatoes.

Roast for at least one hour. Tomato tops will start to crinkle and blacken (caramelize).

Take out of the oven and let rest until the pan is no longer volcanically hot. Then blend the tomatoes in batches. You'll have a large batch of soup, so cool the leftovers, then ladle into freezer bags. Lay the bags flat on top of each other on a cooking sheet to freeze. Once solid, they will stack nicely in your freezer.

FIRST-PLACE CHILI

Katie Brown
Home Chef
Berea, OH

"   I grew up with meat at every dinner, and loads of butter courtesy of my first-generation Ukranian and Irish parents. In the isolated rural villages where my grandparents came from, it was 'add the cream, save the fat, and throw in the bones!' Never in a million years would I have imagined vegan cooking as something I would do. But fast-forward to adulthood—I married a vegetarian, and we have a son with egg/dairy allergies, so here we are.

This chili recipe won the top prize at a friend's chili cook-off, beating out all the meat-based traditional versions. Plan ahead and make this the day before. The chili is best when it simmers overnight."

Serves 8

INGREDIENTS

2–3 tablespoons olive oil

1 large onion, finely chopped

4–5 garlic cloves, minced

2 large carrots, grated

4 cups vegetable broth

2 (28-ounce) cans of whole or diced tomatoes

1 green pepper, diced

3 cans dark red kidney beans, rinsed and drained

3 cans black beans, rinsed and drained

3 celery stalks, finely chopped

1 can corn

3 tablespoons chili powder

3 tablespoons cumin

2 teaspoons salt (or to taste)

1 teaspoon pepper (or to taste)

2 tablespoons sriracha

INSTRUCTIONS

In a large pot, sauté the onions and celery in the olive oil until the onion is translucent.

Add half the cumin and half the chili powder (1 tablespoon each) and cook for another minute.

Add the garlic and cook for two minutes.

Add the vegetable broth and bring to a simmer.

Puree the tomatoes in a blender (a few quick pulses will do) and add to the pot.

Add the rest of the chili powder and cumin, the salt, pepper, and siracha.

Keep the heat at a simmer and add the peppers and carrots.

Add the beans and corn.

Simmer over low heat all night. The longer it simmers, the better.

LOW & SLOW BLACK BEANS

Kelly Wright
Restaurant Owner | Borderline Cafe
Lakewood, OH
borderlinecafe.com
Facebook: @borderlinecafe

"I started my restaurant with my sister Carrie when we were in our early twenties. We wanted to bring a Tex-Mex style of breakfast food to Cleveland because no one was really doing it here yet. Over the years, we've formed a loyal following, keeping it small, keeping it in the family, and forming decade-long friendships with our customers.

These black beans are a foundation ingredient for us. Use them to fill burritos or tacos, serve them over rice, or eat them alone topped with fresh cilantro and tomatoes. The key is the long cook time, so start your beans soaking when you get home from the bar on Saturday night, get them on the stove when you wake up, and by the time halftime rolls around, you'll be ready to go."

Serves 8-10

INGREDIENTS

1 pound black beans

2 cloves garlic

1 diced onion

1 teaspoon salt

1 teaspoon black pepper

1 teaspoon smoked paprika

1 tablespoon cumin

1 tablespoon chili powder

INSTRUCTIONS

Sort and soak one pound of dried black beans overnight.

The next day, drain and rinse.

Fill the pot with fresh water, add the garlic and onion, and bring to a boil.

Turn down heat, simmer for a minimum of two hours or until the beans are soft.

Purée with an immersion blender, or mash with a potato masher, to desired consistency.

Stir in spices, adjust to taste.

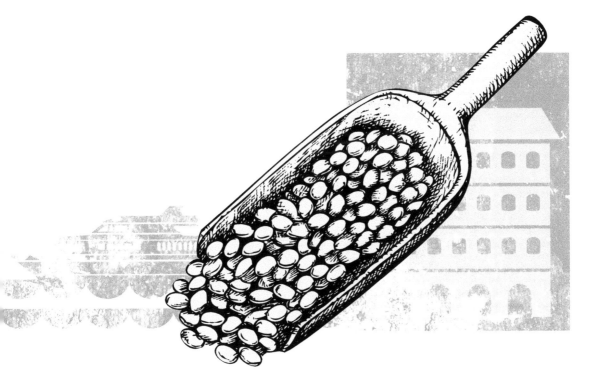

ITALIAN ROASTED VEGETABLE SANDWICH

Kelly Wright

Restaurant Owner | Borderline Cafe
Lakewood, OH
borderlinecafe.com
Facebook: @borderlinecafe

You will not miss the cheese. Not all sandwiches require cheese. Do not add cheese. Let the vegetables do the work. Do not go through all this delicate caring and appreciation for your vegetables and then insult them by adding cheese.

Serves 2

INGREDIENTS

For the filling:

1 cup sliced cremini mushrooms

1 seeded, sliced zucchini

1 seeded, sliced red pepper

1 sliced sweet onion

1/2 cup jarred banana peppers with brine

Generous drizzle of balsamic vinegar

Generous drizzle of olive oil

For the dressing:

Handful of fresh basil

1 tablespoon olive oil

1 very ripe avocado

1 teaspoon oregano

1/2 teaspoon rosemary

1/2 teaspoon thyme

1/4 teaspoon minced garlic

1/2 cup of your favorite pizza or marinara sauce

1 large or 2 smaller baguettes (toasted)

Crushed red pepper to taste

INSTRUCTIONS

Preheat the oven to 375°F.

In a large bowl, combine the vegetables, balsamic vinegar, and olive oil.

Spread veggies on a baking sheet and roast until caramelized, 25–30 minutes or so.

Purée a handful of fresh basil with the olive oil.

Mash the avocado with the spices.

Mix the avocado and puréed basil.

Split and toast/broil a baguette.

Slather one side of the baguette with the basil avocado dressing and the other side with the marinara.

Pile on the veggies, hit them with some red pepper flakes, split the sandwich, and share it with someone you love.

CHICKPEA & GREEN PEA FALAFEL

Shelley Freed
Home Chef
Shaker Heights, OH

"   Like the rest of the world, I cooked my way through the pandemic of 2020. That same year, my daughter decided to eat vegan, so we added new meals to our regular rotation. I learned quickly how to stock my fridge and cupboards with chia seeds, oat milk, and tofu, and learned to cook and season a lot of new things. I try and modify new recipes regularly. (I think that vegan chocolate pudding made with oat milk is sooo much better with some cayenne pepper!) I've been known on occasion to use dinner party guests as my test kitchen guinea pigs. This recipe is a staple for us."

Chef's Note: These can also be fried. I bake them for less oil, less mess, and for efficiency. I soak and cook my own beans because I like to control the amount of salt and I think that the texture is better, but canned beans work fine, too. I usually double or triple this recipe, because it lasts well in a sealed, refrigerated container and is great for snacks.

Serves 4

INGREDIENTS

1 cup canned chickpeas, drained

3/4 cup frozen peas, defrosted

1/4 red onion, coarsely chopped

2 cloves garlic

1/2 cup parsley leaves

1 1/2 tablespoons lemon juice

1 teaspoon cumin

1 teaspoon salt

1/2 teaspoon black pepper

1/4 teaspoon red pepper flakes

2 tablespoons almond flour (regular flour can be substituted for almond flour)

1 teaspoon baking soda

For serving: pita bread, cucumbers, tomatoes

INSTRUCTIONS

Preheat the oven to 375°F.

Coarsely chop all ingredients and pulse in a food processor. You want it to be a little chunky, not a paste. Taste and adjust seasoning if necessary.

Scoop out by a heaping tablespoon and form into small balls. Place on a parchment paper-lined baking sheet.

Bake for 25 minutes. Carefully flip with a spatula and cook for another 20 minutes.

Serve in a pita sandwich with tomatoes and cucumber, or as a main dish over a salad. Serve hot or at room temperature. Leftovers are delicious when toasted in a skillet to reheat.

EGGPLANT & LENTIL BURGER

Jodi Berg
CEO | Vitamix
North Olmsted, OH
Recipe by the Vitamix culinary team

" This is a lovely vegan burger where the patty is made in the Vitamix creating the perfect consistency of lentils and eggplant. Carrot, celery, and onion are used to flavor a stock for the lentils, which are then blended together, not wasting anything. Burgers can be made ahead of time and frozen for a quick, easy, and healthy vegan dinner. Garnish these burgers with your favorite toppings—relish, roasted red peppers, and arugula are all great."

 RBVK Tip: If you don't have a Vitamix, you can use a food processor.

Makes 6 burgers

INGREDIENTS

1/2 cup lentils

4 sprigs fresh thyme leaves

1/2 carrot, quartered

1 celery stalk, quartered

1/2 small red onion, halved

1 small eggplant

2 portobello mushrooms, gills cleaned, quartered

3 cloves garlic

1/2 teaspoon smoked paprika

1/4 cup fresh cilantro leaves, chopped

1/4 cup fresh mint leaves, chopped

1/4 cup flat leaf parsley, finely chopped

1/4 cup bread crumbs, or chickpea crumbs

1 teaspoon pomegranate molasses

1/4 teaspoon salt, optional

2 tablespoons olive oil, optional

INSTRUCTIONS

Preheat oven to 375°F.

Place carrot, celery, and red onion in the Vitamix container and secure the lid. Select variable 4 and pulse 5–6 times until ingredients are uniformly chopped.

Using a spatula, scrape chopped vegetable mix into a small saucepot, add the lentils and fresh thyme leaves, and cover with water. Add salt and simmer for 20–25 minutes or until lentils are soft.

Roughly chop the eggplant and sprinkle with 1/2 teaspoon of salt. Let sit for 10 minutes to allow excess moisture to release. Pat dry and spread the eggplant on a large baking sheet with the mushrooms and garlic. Sprinkle with paprika and roast for 20 minutes or until tender.

Drain the lentil mixture and leave to steam dry while the vegetables are roasting. Pick the fresh thyme sprigs out of the lentils and discard.

Place the eggplant mixture and the lentil mixture into the Vitamix container and secure the lid. Start the blender on its lowest speed, then quickly increase to its highest speed. Blend for 20–30 seconds, using the tamper to press ingredients toward the blades. The mixture should be smooth; for more texture in your burger, blend for less time.

Scrape into a mixing bowl and add the bread crumbs, pomegranate molasses, and herbs. Mix to combine. Portion into 6 patties and place in the refrigerator to chill for at least an hour.

To cook, place a nonstick pan over medium-high heat, and add just enough oil to coat the bottom of the pan. Add the burgers and cook for 3 minutes on each side, then place in the oven for 5 minutes or until heated through. Or, place burgers on a parchment- or silicone-lined baking tray and bake for 12–15 minutes or until heated through.

FISHLESS TACOS

Eric Obenauf

Publisher/ Book Store & Cafe Owner | Two Dollar Radio
Columbus, OH
twodollarradio.com

" A solid A+ drum solo, these fish tacos will trigger the sound of flip-flops spanking sand-dimpled heels, and scratchy salsa music trumpeting from an old boombox."

This recipe is from indie publisher Two Dollar Radio's *Two Dollar Radio's Guide to Vegan Cooking* by Jean-Claude van Randy and Speed Dog (with Eric Obenauf). Eric Obenauf and his wife, Eliza, founded their publishing company in 2005, which now includes their brick-and-mortar indie bookstore and vegan cafe at Two Dollar Radio Headquarters in Columbus.

Serves 4

INGREDIENTS

1 cup plant-based milk of your choosing

1/2 cup lemon juice

1 tablespoon caper juice

1 eggplant, peeled

Zest of 1 lemon

1 tablespoon salt

1 teaspoon Creole seasoning

2 cups flour

Oil for frying

Warm tortillas for serving

Favorite taco toppings for serving: shredded lettuce, tomatoes, salsa, etc.

INSTRUCTIONS

Peel the eggplant and slice top-to-bottom into long 1/2-inch diameter strips.

Add flour, spices, milk, and caper and lemon juice to mixing bowl and stir. Add water slowly until batter resembles a thick pancake batter.

Coat eggplant in batter.

Fry in pan.

Chef's Note: Put these fishless filets on burritos, tacos, or serve as fish and chips with a cheap, crisp lager and a game of horseshoes. If you've got the time, whip up this chimichurri sauce.

CHIMICHURRI SAUCE

In a blender, blend:

3/4 cup oil

1/3 cup apple cider vinegar

1 teaspoon crushed red pepper

1 teaspoon salt

1 bunch diced parsley

2 bunch diced cilantro

5–7 pieces garlic

RBVK Tip: Miss the Friday night Lenten fish fry in your local church basement? Fry up these filets and pair them with John Hagerty's Mac and Cheese (p. 84) and Chef Chaundrea's fries and coleslaw (p. 80). Make vegan tartar sauce by adding some relish and mustard to homemade mayo ("Make It/Buy It" p. 21).

CLEVELAND-STYLE POLISH BOY

Chef Chaundrea

Professional Chef | Shea Culinary Services
Cleveland, OH
eatshea.com
Instagram: @wrapitupshea

" A Polish boy is traditionally a sausage sandwich topped with french fries, barbecue sauce, and coleslaw. As a child, making Polish boys was always an event. My mom would buy special buns and go all out. When I became vegan, I missed the familiar taste of these delicious sandwiches. It can be difficult to find a vegan version, but this one satisfies that tangy, tasty craving."

Serves 4

INGREDIENTS

8 vegan sausages (I prefer the Field Roast brand)

8 hoagie buns

Barbecue Sauce:

1 cup ketchup

1/2 cup Adagio Chocolate Chai Tea (or any black tea that you prefer, or try coffee if you're not a tea person)

1/4 cup apple cider vinegar

1/3 cup brown sugar

1 tablespoon dijon mustard

1 teaspoon salt

1/4 teaspoon black pepper

Coleslaw:

1 head green cabbage, shredded

1 head red cabbage, shredded

1 carrot, shredded

1 cup vegan mayo

1/4 cup sugar

2 tablespoons salt

2 teaspoons pepper

1/2 teaspoon celery seed

1/4 cup apple cider vinegar

Fries:

Russet potatoes

Salt

INSTRUCTIONS

Make the sauce: Bring wet ingredients to a simmer in a saucepan. Add dry ingredients, and then cook for 20 minutes, stirring occasionally.

Make the coleslaw: While barbecue sauce is simmering, put cabbage in a large bowl. Add the rest of the ingredients and massage into the cabbage. Let stand for 5 minutes. You can let it sit for longer to improve the flavor!

Make the fries: Cut the potatoes into fries. In a deep pan or stovetop pot, heat oil to 320°F. Cook fries in the hot oil for 5 minutes and allow to cool. Keep the oil on the stove (you're going to toss the fries back in after you cook the sausage).

Cook the sausages: Cook vegan sausage in a skillet on the stove. Toast buns in the oven for a few minutes.

Increase fry oil heat to 360ºF and cook for an additional 5 minutes. Remove fries, drain, and toss in salt and pepper.

Assemble: Place sausage in bun, add fries. Add a scoop of coleslaw and top with barbecue sauce.

Chef's Notes: You can bake the fries, just place them in the oven before you start the BBQ sauce. You can also use a preshredded coleslaw mix, if you like.

DETROIT-STYLE CONEY DOG

 RBVK Tip: Cleveland's not the only one with its own dog. Enter into the ring the Detroit-style coney dog! It's a little simpler, so you don't need a full recipe (sorry Detroiters). Instead of the toppings above, all you need to do is top your dog (steamed, not grilled) with your favorite chili, mustard, and diced, raw white onions. Amy's brand chili in a can is pretty decent for this, but if you prefer homemade, flip to p. 66 for the First-Place Chili recipe. Traditionally, Detroit dogs call for a no-bean, beef chili, but the RBVK believes in the rights of beans to exist in all chilis!

CASSEROLES
OLES
& SiDES

MAC & CHEESE

John Hagerty
Professional Chef
Cleveland, OH
Instagram: @chefjohnhagerty, @clecheesecakeco

" I've been a chef for fifteen years. I've worked in Cleveland most of my career. I was interested in cooking vegan food when I noticed there just weren't really any great options. It was also a challenge for me to learn new ingredients and techniques—I liked that. In 2021, I opened the (100 percent vegan) Green Kitchen at the Little Rose Tavern. I also make vegan cheesecakes for the Cleveland Cheesecake Company."

RUST BELT VEGAN KITCHEN

Serves 6

INGREDIENTS

1 pound cavatappi pasta

1 1/2 medium carrots, diced

1/2 potato, diced

1/2 yellow onion, diced

1/2 red bell pepper, seeded and diced

1 cup raw cashews

4 whole garlic cloves

1 1/2 cups nutritional yeast

1/2 can unsweetened coconut milk

1 1/2 tablespoons kosher salt

1/4 tablespoon coarse ground black pepper

1 tablespoon paprika

1/2 tablespoon hot sauce

1/2 teaspoon turmeric

2 cups water (more or less as needed)

Juice of 1/2 lemon

INSTRUCTIONS

Cook your pasta according to the package instructions.

Combine all the ingredients except for the nutritional yeast into a large saucepan or pot. Simmer for 20 minutes or until cashews and veggies are tender.

Stir in the nutritional yeast and let it simmer another minute or so as it dissolves.

Puree with a high-speed blender or stick blender. The sauce should be loose with a velvety texture. If the sauce seems too thick, stir in more water slowly until desired consistency is reached.

Season with more salt, pepper, and hot sauce to taste.

Pour over the cooked pasta and gently stir. Start with 2 cups, then add more to desired level of sauciness. Save the remaining sauce for for dipping pretzels, pouring over vegetables, or making nachos.

 RBVK Tip: Store leftover mac in the refrigerator, then reheat leftovers on the stove, stirring in a bit of plant-based milk and leftover sauce for moisture. Reheating in the oven or microwave will dry it out too much, and the beauty of this recipe is that creamy, velvety sauce.

POTATO, SAUERKRAUT, & APPLE CASSEROLE

Renate Jakupca

Professional Chef | ARK in Berea Eco-Museum
Berea, OH
theicea.com

"My husband David and I are the owners of the ARK (Architektur Recycled Kulturstall) in Berea, Ohio, which is a historic eco-museum. We were concerned about the loss of Old World recipes and began searching for the ones our *omas* (grandmothers) made back in Germany. We've found many as a result of our research and hope to publish these recipes in our own cookbook soon.

This vegan potato sauerkraut casserole is a warm, cozy, and filling dish that we love to feed our family and friends at the museum. It was originally a recipe handed down from my grandma that we altered by simply omitting the meat. There's plenty of Old World flavor left in this dish!"

Serves 6

INGREDIENTS

Oil for sautéing

4–5 cups potatoes, diced to 1/2-inch cubes (Yukon Gold work well)

3–4 cups apples, diced to 1/2-inch cubes (tart apples are best, like Granny Smith)

2 cups sweet onion, diced to 1/4" pieces

2 (14-ounce) containers sauerkraut; fresh is best, but canned will work (not drained)

1–2 teaspoons favorite seasoning salt, optional

1 teaspoon caraway seeds, crushed, optional

INSTRUCTIONS

Preheat the oven to 425°F.

Place potatoes in a bowl of cold water and set aside.

Sauté onions in oil, using a splash of vegetable broth or water to loosen stuck bits of onion as they brown, scraping the pan as you splash the liquid in.

Using your hands, assemble the layers in a casserole dish in this order: potatoes, apples, sauerkraut (including the juice), onions, seasoning.

Cover with foil and bake for 1 hour. Uncover and continue to bake for 15 minutes or until browned on top.

Serve with your favorite mustard. I love it with horseradish Dijon.

WHATEVER'S AVAILABLE STUFFED SQUASH

Jamie Gentry
Home Chef | Food Pantry Volunteer Chef
Chicago, IL

" I am a home chef turned volunteer chef and team-lead at a local food pantry and community kitchen, Ravenswood Community Services (RCS), in Chicago, Illinois. Every Tuesday, our tiny basement on Wilson Avenue cranks out more than 250 hot, healthy, and free meals for patrons of the food pantry. Though it's certainly been challenging at times, I am immensely proud of each and every meal we've made—not once have we sacrificed flavor or ambition or failed to make good use of produce surprises or surpluses.

When it's our turn to design a meal, my dear friend Kelly and I comb the pantry shelves to see what surprise surplus of produce we'll be working with that week. Sometimes we'll receive 2,000 pounds of fresh, colorful produce like bell peppers, summer squash, and multicolored carrots. Other weeks we'll receive 1,000 pounds of sweet potatoes and six boxes of pears. With a small budget to supplement the pantry offerings, menu planning requires an exceptional amount of creativity in order to accommodate a variety of age groups, dietary restrictions, and taste preferences. We strive to create interesting, protein and vegetable-heavy meals that fill our neighbors' bellies as well as their hearts.

This recipe was developed as part of a food education program to help squash-curious patrons of Chicago food pantries explore the possibilities of incorporating the fruit (it's a fruit!) into their meals. The emphasis of this particular recipe is on produce or pantry staples that are regularly available, but it can be easily adapted to whatever a home chef might have in their cupboards."

Makes 4 side servings or 2 mains

INGREDIENTS

2 acorn squash

For the filling: makes about 3 cups of filling

1 cup of protein (tofu or other plant-based protein)*

2 cups roasted vegetables (onions, garlic, mushrooms, zucchini, bell peppers, zucchini, etc.)**

1/2 cup cooked grains (rice, beans, or quinoa)

1–3 teaspoons herbs or spices (paprika, smoked paprika, thyme, oregano, curry powder)

2 tablespoons Dijon mustard, optional

1/2 cup dried fruit and/or nuts (cranberries, cherries, almonds, walnuts, pecans), optional

Olive oil

Salt

Pepper

INSTRUCTIONS

Arrange oven rack to lower-middle position and heat oven to 375°F. Cut the squash in half from stem to root and scoop out the seeds.***

Put a little olive oil on the orange flesh of the squash and place it flesh-side down into a baking dish or onto a parchment-lined baking sheet. Roast for 30–50 minutes, depending on the size of your squash. You'll know the squash is ready to come out of the oven when you can easily push a fork into it.

While the squash is baking, prepare the filling by sautéing the vegetables in olive oil on medium heat, or roasting them (see note below). Season to taste with spices, salt, and pepper. Set aside in a large bowl.

Bring the squash out of the oven and place flesh-side up on a clean baking sheet or plate. Your squash halves will look like bowls. Scoop out a little of the interior of the squash bowls, leaving enough to give the bowl some structure so that it doesn't collapse before you fill it.

Add the scooped squash to your prepared filling.

Add the cooked grains and protein.

Add in dried fruit, nuts, and mustard (if using), and stir with a wooden spoon or spatula until combined.

Divide the filling mixture between the squash halves (really pile it in there!) and bake for 15–20 minutes.

Chef's Notes:

* You can buy baked and seasoned tofu or plant-based protein (dehydrated textured vegetable protein, veggie "crumbles" in the freezer section) in most grocery stores.

**Evenly chop the vegetables you have on hand, lightly coat in olive oil, and place on a baking sheet to roast in your oven at 400°F. Roast for 20–30 min, depending on the vegetable and your preferred level of roast/tenderness.

***Toast your squash seeds! Squash seeds make a tasty snack and/or topping for your meal. Place pulpy seeds in a bowl or colander and use water to pull the squash pulp away from the seeds. Dry clean seeds on a towel in an even layer for at least 30 minutes. Toss dry seeds with salt, pepper (or other desired seasonings), and a little bit of olive oil. Place them in a single layer on a baking sheet lined with parchment. Bake for 15–20 min or until golden brown at 275°F. Cool before eating.

JIFFY CORN CASSEROLE

Linda Zolten Wood
Home Chef
Cleveland, OH

" Updated family traditions are easier with such good replacements. My grandma made traditional corn casserole for Thanksgiving and it was a favorite. I missed it dearly when I went vegan, so I created this version. Don't skip the skillet step for that delicious brown crust. If you have leftovers, slice and freeze with waxed paper in between layers of slices."

Serves 6–8

INGREDIENTS

2 boxes vegetarian corn muffin mix (I recommend "Vegetarian" Jiffy. The original "America's Favorite" Jiffy has animal lard in it.)

2 cups salted plant-based butter, melted

4 tablespoons aquafaba

16 ounces sour cream alternative (I like the Kite Hill brand)

2 (14-ounce) cans of corn, drained

2 (14-ounce) cans creamed corn

INSTRUCTIONS

Preheat oven to 350°F.

Line two 9 x12-inch or similar size pans with parchment paper.

In a large bowl, mix all the ingredients well.

Bake for 1 hour and 20 minutes, or until a toothpick can be cleanly removed.

Let cool enough to cut into squares.

For a browned, caramelized crust, toast the squares in a skillet with plant-based butter.

GRAN'S GREEN BEAN SALAD

Heather Donaldson
Professional Chef | Mad Cheese, LLC
Cincinnati, OH
madcheesecincy.com
Facebook: @madcheesecincy
Instagram: @madcheesecincy

"This was originally my great-grandmother's recipe. My great-grandparents (Gran and Pa) immigrated from Germany and lived in New Bremen, Ohio. My father remembers going to their house for lunch every other Saturday. More often than not, this salad was on the table.

Pa was a physician and had a custom hutch built for his office in the 1920s. He stored medications on the shelves and files and instruments in the drawers. I now have the hutch and use it in my kitchen—spices on the shelves and cookware and other ingredients in the drawers. My grandmother (their daughter-in-law) lived in Dayton, Ohio. I was very close to her and spent a lot of time at her house. I remember making this salad with her in her kitchen. Make it a day before you plan to serve it so it chills overnight and the dressing can really marinate the vegetables."

Serves 4-6

INGREDIENTS

1 pound fresh green beans, washed and trimmed

1 large yellow onion, sliced into thin rounds

1 cup raw cashews, soaked overnight or boiled for 30 minutes

1/3 cup water

2 tablespoons lemon juice

1 teaspoon apple cider vinegar

1/2 teaspoon sea salt

1/4 cup sugar

1 1/2 tablespoons white vinegar

INSTRUCTIONS

Steam the green beans until they are just tender but still bright green.

Drain and rinse the cashews and add to a blender along with the water, lemon juice, vinegar, and sea salt. Blend until creamy and smooth, stopping to scrape down the sides as needed. Add the sugar and white vinegar and blend briefly to incorporate.

In a loaf pan or casserole dish, create a single layer of green beans, followed by a single layer of onion slices. Sprinkle with coarse sea salt. Spoon about a third of the cashew cream over the layer and spread to cover evenly. Repeat the layering process until all ingredients have been used. Cover and refrigerate overnight.

 RBVK Tip: Our test kitchen made a double batch of the cashew dressing. Some blenders will blend better with more volume in the container, and you want the dressing to be smooth, not chunky. The dressing is so delicious, you'll use up the extra very quickly. It's sweet, so it makes a great dip for fruit.

SWISS CHARD AND POTATOES (BLITVA)

Joe Valencic
Home Chef
Cleveland, OH

" Blitva is a popular side dish along the Adriatic coast of Slovenia and Croatia. Some Slovenian cooks, like my mother, substitute spinach for the chard. Similar dishes include English bubble-and-squeak (with cabbage) and Irish colcannon (with kale).

Recipes can take you back to a favorite place or time. This is one of the simple, traditional dishes my mother prepared when I was growing up. It also reminds me of meals with friends and family in Europe."

Serves 6–8

INGREDIENTS

2 pounds Swiss chard (red chard works best)

3–4 medium yellow potatoes, peeled and diced

2–3 garlic cloves, minced

2–3 tablespoons olive oil

Pinch of red pepper flakes, optional

Salt and pepper to taste

INSTRUCTIONS

Bring to a boil a large pot of salted water. Add potatoes.

Rinse the chard and remove tough stems. Tear into large pieces or cut into half-inch strips.

When the potatoes are nearly done, add the chard. Cook together for 10 minutes.

In a large pan, sauté the garlic in olive oil. Season the oil and garlic with salt and pepper and add red pepper flakes, if desired. Drain the cooked chard and potatoes and add to the pan. Stir and cook for 1 minute to blend flavors.

The well-cooked potatoes will take on a creamy texture. For a thicker, soup-like texture, add some of the cooking water.

Hearty
MAIN
DISHES

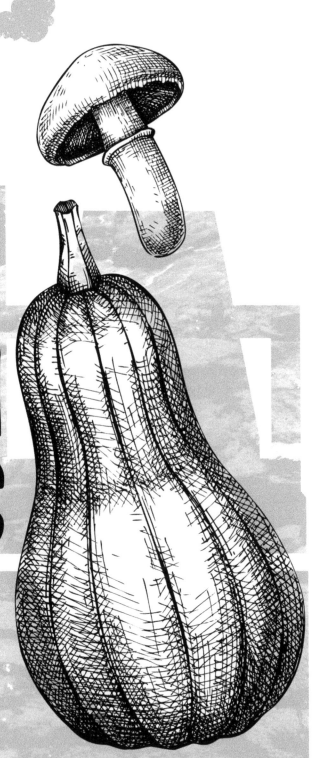

CINCINNATI CHILI

Shantini Gamage
Home Chef
Cincinnati, OH

" I grew up in Ontario, Canada, in a family of Sri Lankan and Malaysian customs. One of my fondest memories is of large family get-togethers on weekends with lots of laughing and cooking and eating. It instilled in me a love for experimenting with flavors and with entertaining. School and life brought me to the Midwest, and I've now lived in Cincinnati longer than I've lived any other place. Cincinnati-style chili took me a while to get used to when I first moved here. Cinnamon and cloves in chili? And served on spaghetti? No thanks! But I do love pasta, and the Mediterranean flavors of the chili reminded me of curries. It was only a matter of time before I was a convert. When I transitioned to being vegan, I strived to replicate the flavors and textures of traditional beef-based Cincinnati chili to suit my new diet. After a few trials, I think I figured it out. Even my meat-eating husband loves it! I encourage you to try this unique Cincinnati dish. It's perfect for get-togethers large and small."

Chef's Notes: The cheddar that is used for authentic Cincinnati-style chili is shredded into very fine strands and mounded on top of the serving of spaghetti and chili. For a vegan substitute, shred a block of vegan cheddar cheese (preferably with a fine-holed grater) or use preshredded cheddar cheese.

The lentil-quinoa mixture in this recipe will weigh about 2 pounds. You can use a similar weight of purchased plant-based ground beef substitute instead of the lentil-quinoa mixture if you prefer or if you're short on time.

I prefer to add the kidney beans to the chili after the vinegar and chocolate, but this is not traditional for Cincinnati-style chili. And I don't do this if serving the chili to native Cincinnatians!

Serves 8

INGREDIENTS

For the lentil-quinoa ground meat substitute:

1 cup dried brown lentils, cooked in water and drained

1 cup dried red quinoa, cooked in water and drained

1/3 cup nutritional yeast

1 tablespoon coconut aminos (or liquid aminos)

1 teaspoon smoked paprika

For the chili base:

1 tablespoon olive oil

2 medium onions, chopped finely

1 tablespoon garlic, chopped very finely

1/3 cup chili powder

1 teaspoon ground cinnamon

1 teaspoon ground cumin

1/2 teaspoon ground cloves

1/4 teaspoon ground allspice

1/2 teaspoon ground cayenne or other hot red pepper, or more to taste

2 bay leaves

2 cups canned tomato sauce

4 cups vegan no-beef broth (vegetable broth can be used if you cannot find
  vegan no-beef broth)

2 tablespoons apple cider vinegar

1 ounce unsweetened chocolate

Salt to taste

For serving:

1 pound spaghetti, cooked

4 ounces vegan shredded cheddar cheese

1 (15-ounce) can red kidney beans, drained, rinsed, and warmed

1 small onion, diced

Vegan oyster crackers

Mild hot sauce

INSTRUCTIONS

To make the ground meat substitute, mix the cooked lentils and the cooked quinoa in a large bowl.

In a food processor, grind two-thirds of this lentil-quinoa mixture to a rough paste (about 6 pulses) and transfer it back to the bowl with the unground mixture.

Add the nutritional yeast, paprika, and coconut aminos. Mix well to combine all ingredients and set aside.

To make the chili base, heat the olive oil in a medium saucepan over medium heat. Add the chopped onion and cook until soft but not browned, about 3 or 4 minutes.

Add the garlic and cook, stirring, until fragrant, about 30 seconds. Add the chili powder, cinnamon, cumin, cloves, allspice, and cayenne and stir for about 30 seconds.

Add the tomato sauce and bay leaf and stir. Bring to a simmer and cook for about 2 minutes.

To combine the base and other chili ingredients, you'll need a large pot. Add the broth and the lentil-quinoa ground meat substitute mixture to the pot, breaking up the mixture as it is added.

Bring the mixture to a boil and then reduce to a simmer, stirring to break up the lentil-quinoa mixture further until it is uniform in the liquid. Add the chili base mixture from your saucepan to the large pot. Mix well. Let simmer for 30 minutes, stirring occasionally.

Add the vinegar and chocolate to the pot and stir until the chocolate is melted and combined into chili.

Add salt to taste and stir. Remove the bay leaves.

To serve the chili, place cooked spaghetti on a plate and top with the chili. Add the vegan cheese, kidney beans, and chopped onions on top as desired. Serve with oyster crackers and mild hot sauce on the side.

Chef's Note: In Cincinnati lingo, a "two-way" is spaghetti with chili on top, a "three-way" has shredded cheddar cheese added on top of the two-way, a "four-way" has diced onions or kidney beans added to the three-way, and a "five-way" has diced onions and kidney beans added to the three-way.

BLACK BEAN PICADILLO

Teresa Stone
Home Chef
Loveland, OH

" Growing up, food was an event in my family: something to be planned, discussed, looked forward to, and savored. Dinner was truly the highlight of each day. In my childhood, meals were steeped in American midwestern traditions. But, after becoming vegetarian in the 1980s and then vegan in the late 1990s, I was compelled to look outward toward other cuisines for inspiration and create my own repertoire of favorite dishes. The type of food I now enjoy may differ from what I was accustomed to when I was young, but I am still firmly rooted in a passion for cooking, recipes, and ingredients, just like my mother.

The recipe presented here evolved after reading about Cuban picadillo. Picadillo is a stewy, spiced hash typically composed of ground pork or beef. In my version, black beans are the perfect stand-in for the meat. There are sweet notes from the fruit, salty elements from the olives, warmth from the cinnamon and cumin, and an underlying brightness from the wine and vinegar. This dish has been a staple in my family since my children were toddlers. My son, now in college, has incorporated Black Bean Picadillo into his own cooking repertoire. This recipe is truly worthy of being passed down from mother to son."

Serves 4-6

INGREDIENTS

4 tablespoons olive oil

2 medium onions, peeled and diced

1 green or red pepper, cored, seeded, and diced

6 cloves garlic, peeled and minced

1 teaspoon dried thyme

1 teaspoon dried oregano

2 teaspoons ground cumin*

1 teaspoon ground coriander*

1/2 teaspoon ground cinnamon

1/8 teaspoon cayenne pepper

2 bay leaves

2 tablespoons tomato paste

1/3 cup dry white or red wine** or water

4 cans black beans, drained and rinsed

1 (14 1/2-ounce) can diced tomatoes

1/2 cup golden raisins

3/4 cup large pimento-stuffed green olives, drained and sliced

1 cup peeled and diced mango***

2 teaspoons red wine vinegar

Salt and pepper

White rice, cooked according to package instructions, for serving

Chef's Notes:

* McCormick Gourmet offers a line of pre-roasted spices. I recommend roasted cumin and roasted coriander because they are richer and more flavorful than their unroasted counterparts.

** Consult barnivore.com to ensure that your wine is vegan.

*** I prefer Champagne mangoes (also called Ataulfo or honey mangoes) for their fiberless flesh, and I often incorporate them into savory dishes.

INSTRUCTIONS

Heat olive oil in a large skillet over medium-high heat until the oil shimmers. Add onions; stir and sauté for 5 minutes.

Add the bell pepper to the onions and cook, stirring occasionally, for about 15 minutes until the onion is translucent and starting to turn golden in color.

Add the garlic, herbs, and spices (thyme through bay leaves). Stirring continuously, sauté for 2 minutes.

Clear a spot in the middle of the pan by pushing the vegetables to the side and add the tomato paste. Mash the tomato paste around with your spoon; let it sizzle for a few seconds, then incorporate it into the vegetables. While constantly stirring for about 2 minutes, watch as the mixture turns darker in color, almost brick red.

Add the wine or water in order to deglaze—the caramelized tomato paste will release from the pan. Let the liquid reduce for 2 minutes.

Add beans, tomatoes, and raisins. Simmer uncovered for 5 minutes.

Add the olives, mango, and vinegar. Cook for 5 minutes more. Turn off the stove burner. Season with salt and pepper to taste.

Serve over cooked white rice.

CAULIFLOWER & CHICKPEA MASALA

Joel Tishken
Home Chef
Richmond, IN

"   A masala refers to a particular spice blend from South Asian cuisines. There are many varieties of dishes featuring masala spices. This one includes cauliflower, chickpea, onion, and tomato."

Serves 4

INGREDIENTS

1/2 head cauliflower, chopped bite size

1 can chickpeas, drained (or the dried and cooked equivalent)

2 medium fresh tomatoes, diced

1 medium onion, diced

1 1/2 tablespoons canola or olive oil

1 teaspoon salt

1 teaspoon black pepper

1/2 teaspoon curry powder

1/2 teaspoon ground cumin

2 teaspoons garam masala

Rice, cooked for serving

INSTRUCTIONS

Heat oil in a large skillet over medium-to-high heat.

Fry onion for 5 minutes or so.

Add cauliflower. Cook for at least another 5 minutes or so until both begin to soften and turn golden.

Add salt, pepper, curry powder, cumin, and garam masala. Stir thoroughly to distribute the spices.

Add tomato and chickpeas. Stir again and simmer on low heat for another 5–10 minutes.

The tomatoes will add a bit of liquid to the mixture. You want to serve it wet over the rice, so if it seems dry, add some water or vegetable broth.

MOLE DE XICO ON ROASTED CHAYOTES

Alexandra Iserte-Garcia
Professional Chef | Food Motion
Dublin, OH
Twitter: @foodmotion

" I've been a chef for twenty years. I started my own catering business in Playa del Carmen in 2010 called Food Motion Cooking Workshop. In 2017, I came to Ohio with my husband and child and reopened my project here. I mostly do home cooking classes and catering. I have been in love with vegan cooking since I was introduced to it by my sister-in-law many years ago. In the past few years, I've learned about the benefits that a whole foods, plant-based cuisine can bring to our bodies and how it can help the planet. I want to show people how amazing our cuisine is and that it can easily be made vegan.

Mexican gastronomy is characterized by its lively and pronounced flavors, and this Mole de Xico is no exception. If you can't find these ingredients in your usual grocery store, plan a visit to a local Mexican market."

Serves 8

INGREDIENTS

2 pounds chayotes or zucchini

10 mulato chili peppers

5 pasilla chili peppers

3 ancho chili peppers

1/2 cup of prunes

1 xoconostle, optional (sour prickly pear or cacti fruit)

1 roma tomato, regular size

1 onion

4–5 cups vegetable broth

1/2 cup vegetable oil for frying, plus 2 tablespoons for roasting

Water

1/2 plantain

1/4 cup sesame seeds

1/4 cup pine nuts

1/4 cup raisins

1/4 cup almonds

1/4 cup walnuts

1/4 cup hazelnuts

2 cloves

1 cinnamon stick

20 grams Mexican chocolate (Abuelita)

1 1/2 tablespoons sugar

1/2 teaspoon anise

1 corn tortilla (cut into pieces)

1 slice bread (cut into pieces)

Salt and pepper

INSTRUCTIONS

Preheat the oven at 400° F.

Slice the chayotes lengthwise. Add oil, salt, and pepper and roast them in the oven for 40 minutes. If cooking zucchini instead, roast for just 15 minutes.

Remove the seeds from all the chilies and reserve. In a skillet over medium heat, add 1/2 cup of oil and fry the chilies, stirring occasionally until lightly fried. Make sure to not burn them since they can make the whole sauce bitter.

Transfer the chilis to a bowl, draining with a slotted spoon. Pour enough hot water to cover them, and let them sit for about 15 minutes.

Meanwhile, in the same pan, add the chopped onion and fry for a minute, stirring constantly.

Add the tomato, prunes, sesame, pine nuts, almonds, walnuts, hazelnuts, raisins, the corn tortilla, the bread roll, and a little black pepper. Mix everything and fry for 2–3 minutes or until all the ingredients are lightly fried.

Transfer the ingredients to a bowl and reserve.

Peel and cut the banana and xoconostle. In the same skillet over low heat, pour more oil if needed. Add the banana and xoconostle. Fry for about two minutes and add the cloves, the cinnamon stick, and anise. Fry for one more minute and remove.

In a blender, add the drained chilis, the previous preparation, sugar, broth, and a pinch of salt. Blend well until smooth. Make it in batches if needed.

Add oil to a saucepan and turn on to medium heat. Add the blended mixture, the chocolate bars, and 2 1/2 cups of the broth. Mix and cook over high heat, stirring occasionally. When it boils, lower the heat and cook for half an hour. The idea is that the preparation thickens. Serve hot on top of the roasted chayotes or zucchini.

Top with toasted sesame seeds and a drizzle of vegan plain unsweetened yogurt.

POLENTA WITH MUSHROOM SAUCE

Joe Valencic
Home Chef
Cleveland, OH

When you tire of pasta and rice as the foundation for your vegetable dishes, try making polenta. Here's a simple recipe that combines dried and fresh mushrooms in a rich, savory sauce to top a comforting, warm bowl of polenta.

Serves 4

INGREDIENTS

Polenta:

6 cups salted water

1 3/4 cups yellow cornmeal

Mushroom Sauce:

1 ounce dried porcini mushrooms, chopped

2 tablespoons olive oil

2 tablespoons margarine

1 small onion, finely chopped

1 clove garlic

12 ounces fresh mushrooms, sliced

3 tomatoes, peeled seeded and chopped

Salt and pepper to taste

INSTRUCTIONS

Bring salted water to a boil.

Slowly sprinkle in cornmeal, stirring constantly with a wooden spoon.

Sprinkle very slowly and stir continuously so the cornmeal doesn't form lumps. Continue to stir polenta over low heat until the mixture starts to come away from the sides of the saucepan, 30–40 minutes.

Soak the dried mushrooms in warm water for 10 minutes. Set aside.

Heat oil and margarine in a saucepan. Add onion and whole garlic clove and sauté until onion is golden. Discard garlic.

Drain porcini mushrooms and add the fresh mushrooms to the onions. Cook over medium heat for about 10 minutes, careful to not burn the onions.

Add tomatoes and simmer over low heat for 20 minutes.

Salt and pepper to taste.

To serve, pour polenta into a shallow bowl. Pour the mushroom sauce on the polenta.

POTATO & SAUERKRAUT PIEROGIES

Meredith Pangrace
Home Chef
Cleveland, OH

" Pierogies were in regular rotation for my grandmother's Sunday dinners, but she rarely made her own. She said it wasn't worth the work and Mrs. T's were just as good. She would buy them frozen to sauté with onions and bacon, applesauce and sour cream on the side. While I appreciate knowing what to make from scratch and what to buy, Mrs. T's aren't vegan. It's pretty hard to find any prepared pierogies that are. But the good news is you can make a great pierogi dough on your own, and if you fill them with a premade ingredient (like sauerkraut, or leftover mashed potatoes) it's not as time-consuming as you might think. Make a double batch and freeze them. This recipe calls for half potato-filled and half sauerkraut-filled. I like the surprise of not knowing what I'm going to get when I have several on my plate. You could also mix the sauerkraut into the potatoes and have them all be the same. Once you master the dough and assemblage, get creative with the fillings—caramelized onions, roasted mushrooms, or butternut squash."

Makes about 24 pierogies

INGREDIENTS

Dough:

3 cups flour + flour for dusting work surface

1/2 teaspoon salt

1 cup water

1/2 cup vegan butter, melted

Filling:

2 large potatoes, peeled and cubed

1/2 teaspoon salt

1/2 teaspoon garlic powder

1/2 teaspoon onion powder

1/4 teaspoon black pepper

2 tablespoons plant milk

2 tablespoons nutritional yeast

3 cups sauerkraut, drained

1 medium onion, diced

2 tablespoons oil

INSTRUCTIONS

In a large bowl, combine the flour and salt.

Make a well in the center and pour in the butter and stir.

Slowly add the water and mix. As the dough starts to form, use your hands to knead the dough for about 5 minutes until it's nice and smooth. Cover and let rest while you make the filling.

In a medium pot on the stove, boil the potatoes until tender.

Drain the potatoes and put into a large bowl. Add the salt, spices, milk, and nutritional yeast. Mash, taste for seasoning, adjust, and set aside.

Dust your work surface with flour.

Divide your dough into balls, about the size of a ping-pong ball. You'll get about 2 dozen balls.

Roll out each ball into about a 3-inch circle. Put a spoonful of the potato mixture into the center of half of the circles and fold dough over. Press the edges down with a fork. (You could also try rolling all the dough out flat, and using a glass to cut out the round shapes, if you find that to be quicker.)

Put a spoonful of sauerkraut into the center of the remaining balls and fold dough over. Press the edges down with a fork.

In a large pot, boil the pierogies in salted water for about 5 minutes. Drain. Be gentle so they do not break. Put the ones you're not going to eat immediately into freezer bags.

Brown the onion in olive oil in a large pan over medium heat. Add the pierogies gently and let them brown on one side, then carefully flip to brown the other side.

Salt and pepper to taste. Serve with applesauce and vegan sour cream.

ROASTED CAULIFLOWER WITH ROMESCO SAUCE

Dan Bode
Home Chef
Cleveland, OH

"

When I left college, I started working at the Glidden-Durkee Research Center in Cleveland. I was on the Glidden paint side of the building, but we had access to Durkee spice side, too. The research center felt like the United Nations. People from all over the world worked there, and over lunch, we would talk about how different spices were used in global cuisines, leading to lunches and occasionally dinners at people's homes where they would show off their home country cuisines. I learned a little about traditional uses and began experimenting with blends for my own recipes.

This is not a traditional romesco, but it is rich and flavorful due to the spice mixture. It's great on any grilled vegetables, as a dip for raw vegetables, or even as a sandwich spread."

Serves 2

INGREDIENTS

1 head of cauliflower

1 cup marcona almonds

2 ripe tomatoes, about 1 pound

1 ounce sherry (I recommend Amontillado sherry)

2–4 ounces olive oil

1 teaspoon Spanish paprika

1 teaspoon crushed red pepper flakes

1 teaspoon cumin

1 teaspoon brown mustard seed

Generous pinch of caraway seed

Generous pinch of black pepper

INSTRUCTIONS

Preheat the oven to 400°F.

Roast the cauliflower. For a dramatic presentation, trim and roast the cauliflower whole. Rub it with olive oil and place it in a cast iron skillet. Put a pan of water below it in the oven and roast for about 2 hours. If you have less time, slice the cauliflower, toss in oil, and roast on a cooking sheet for about 45 minutes.

Make the sauce: Crush dry spices in a grinder. (Whole spices you grind yourself will have more intense flavors. If you don't have a spice grinder, you can use a mortar and pestle, or even put the spices in a Ziploc bag and smash with a blunt object!) Blend tomatoes, almonds, half the oil, and sherry, ideally with a high-powered blender like a Vitamix. Add spice mix when blended, adding oil as needed to keep the mixture fluid.

Drizzle the roasted cauliflower with the sauce and serve with extra sauce on the side.

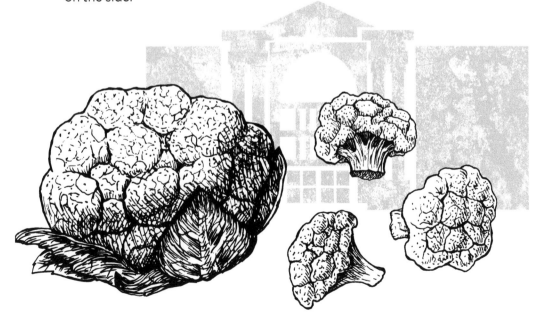

TOFU CHITTERLINGS

Dustin Vanderburg

Professional Chef | Vegan in the Hood
Detroit, MI
Facebook: @veganinthehood
Instagram: @veganinthehoodLLC
Twitter: @Viper2k3sr

"I have always loved cooking. I got started in veganism a handful of years back. I started to miss the options that I had as a kid. We decided to start a restaurant based on the recipes we (my wife and I) enjoyed as kids. We started developing classic dishes from our past like this one, which honors my wife's African American heritage. We also cook dishes like greens, sweet potato casserole, Detroit-style coney dogs, po'boys, and more.

This recipe is part of our soul food collection. My wife and I often make this dish at home."

Serves 6-8

INGREDIENTS

1 pack of large tofu skins, cut into strips*

1 large Vidalia (or yellow sweet) onion, diced

3 large jalapenos, seeded for less heat, sliced

2 large bell peppers, sliced into strips

3 large russet potatoes, sliced

3 ounces Frank's Red Hot Sauce (5 ounces if you want more spice)

2 tablespoons chitterlings seasoning (Spice Supreme brand)

2 tablespoons celery salt

2 tablespoons garlic and pepper seasoning

6 quarts of water (enough to cover vegetables; we use an 11-quart pot)

Chef's Note: You can find tofu skins fresh or dried, we prefer fresh. If you're having trouble finding them in your usual grocery store, visit your local Asian market.

INSTRUCTIONS

Slice and separate the tofu skins into about 1 x 1/2-inch strips and place in the pot.

Place diced onions, peppers, and potatoes in the pot.

Cover with water (about 6 quarts).

Season the pot with the Frank's, celery salt, and other seasonings.

Bring to a boil, and boil for about an hour.

Bring down to a simmer for about 3 hours (until veggies are fork tender).

Serve.

SPLIT PEA CURRY

Austin Walkin' Cane
Home Chef | Blues Musician
Cleveland, OH

Indian comfort food from Kerala to New Dehli, direct to your belly."

Serves 4-6

INGREDIENTS

16 ounces dried split peas

6-8 cups water

3 tablespoons canola oil

1/2 teaspoon black mustard seeds

1 medium onion

1/4 teaspoon turmeric

1/4 teaspoon red pepper

Pinch of chopped cumin

2 chopped dried red chiles

8-10 curry leaves

Splash of white vinegar

Rice for serving

INSTRUCTIONS

Prep the split peas: Add the peas to a pot of boiling water. Boil for two minutes, then cover and let stand for an hour. Drain excess water and set aside.

Boil 6–8 cups of water in a large pot. Add split peas (water should be about 1 inch above split peas). Let the water boil, reduce heat, and partially cover pot.

Simmer for 20–30 minutes until split peas are a desired texture. While the peas are simmering, toast the turmeric and cumin in a pan until you start to smell them. Set aside in a separate dish.

In a separate pan, heat oil at medium-low heat. Add black mustard seeds and dry red chilis. When the seeds start popping, add the onion, curry leaves, red pepper, turmeric, and cumin. Cook until onion starts to brown.

Add your toasted spices, sauteed onions, and spices to your peas.

Add a splash of white vinegar and salt to taste.

Serve over rice.

RED CURRY
WITH VEGETABLES

Elaine Cicora
Home Chef | Food Writer
Cleveland, OH

"After more than two decades as an award-winning restaurant critic, food journalist, and enthusiastic eater, I've sampled more than a little of what the Rust Belt has to offer. I've learned there is one thing you can count on: With our access to locally grown produce, a wide assortment of fine ingredients, and a delightfully diverse population, there is always something good to eat—or to make! Here is a recipe for a savory, Asian-influenced dish I love to cook at home."

Serves 4

INGREDIENTS

4 teaspoons canola oil

1 14-ounce package firm tofu, rinsed, patted dry, and cut into 1-inch cubes

1 pound sweet potatoes, peeled and cut into 1-inch cubes

1 14-ounce can coconut milk

1/2 cup vegetable broth

1 tablespoon red Thai curry paste, or more to taste

1/2 pound of frozen, trimmed greens, thawed but not cooked

1 tablespoon brown sugar

2 teaspoons lime juice

1 teaspoon salt.

1 lime, cut in wedges

INSTRUCTIONS

Heat 2 teaspoons of the oil in a wok over high heat. Add tofu and toss until golden brown. Remove to plate.

Heat remaining oil and add sweet potatoes, tossing until golden brown.

Add coconut milk to wok, along with broth and curry paste. Bring to a boil, then reduce to a simmer.

Cook, covered, stirring occasionally, until the sweet potato is tender.

Add tofu, green beans, and brown sugar. Return to a simmer.

Cook, covered, stirring occasionally, until the green beans are tender-crisp.

Remove from heat, stir in lime juice and salt.

Serve over prepared rice, with lime wedges.

SUMMER PASTA
WITH CREAMY SAUCE

Heather Donaldson

Professional Chef | Mad Cheese, LLC
Cincinnati, OH
madcheesecincy.com
Facebook: @madcheesecincy
Instagram: @madcheesecincy

RUST BELT VEGAN KITCHEN

"

While living in Los Angeles, I started a blog featuring elegant vegan recipes (isntthatthelimit.com). In 2020, my husband and I moved back to Cincinnati (where we both grew up) and bought a home. I stopped working on the blog and started focusing on making vegan cheeses. I launched Mad Cheese, LLC in February of 2021. We create handcrafted, artisan vegan cheeses and charcuterie.

This delicious pasta has a creamy, elegant sauce that is quick, easy, and lower in fat than a dairy or nut-based cream sauce. Hearts of palm get a quick purée in a blender with fresh thyme, garlic, lemon juice, and a bit of olive oil. Adding in some of the water used to cook the pasta makes the sauce glossy and thick. It's delicious on its own, but if you can, add the walnut topping. The salty, cheesy flavor really enhances the sauce and rounds out the dish. You could add any vegetables you like, either boiled with the pasta or quickly steamed or sautéed."

 RBVK Tip: Double or triple the amount of walnut topping you make for this dish to top salads and popcorn.

Serves 4

INGREDIENTS

3 cups dried farfalle or other pasta of choice

2 cups baby spinach, roughly chopped

2 large, ripe tomatoes, roughly chopped

Creamy sauce:

1 can hearts of palm, drained (reserve 1/3 cup of the liquid from the can), roughly chopped

1/3 cup of the water used to boil the pasta

2 tablespoons olive oil

1 teaspoon lemon juice

1 teaspoon fresh thyme leaves, chopped, plus extra thyme leaves for garnish

1/2 teaspoon minced fresh garlic

1/4 teaspoon sea salt

Pinch cayenne

Freshly ground black pepper

Walnut topping:

1/2 cup raw walnuts

1/8 cup nutritional yeast

1/4–1 teaspoon sea salt (depending on strength of salt and personal preference)

INSTRUCTIONS

Make the walnut topping: Combine the walnut topping ingredients in the blender and process until you have a crumb-like consistency. Start with 1/4 teaspoon of sea salt, then taste the mixture and increase the salt to your liking. (I use fine Himalayan sea salt, which tends to be saltier.) Transfer the mixture to a small bowl.

Bring a large pot of heavily salted water to a boil.

Add the pasta and cook according to package directions. During the last couple minutes of cooking, add the spinach to the pot. Do not drain the pasta and spinach using a colander, instead use tongs or a slotted spoon to transfer them to a large bowl.

While the pasta boils, place the sauce ingredients, including the 1/3 cup of liquid from the hearts of palm can, in the blender. (Don't blend yet, just have it ready to go when your pasta is done. You'll be adding some pasta water in the next step.)

Once the pasta is done, transfer 1/3 cup of the cooking water to the blender with the other sauce ingredients. Puree until smooth.

Add the chopped tomato to the large bowl with the pasta and spinach. Pour about 3/4 of the sauce over the pasta and toss to combine.

Divide between four plates, or keep it all in one big serving dish. Drizzle the remaining sauce evenly over the pasta, sprinkle with the walnut topping and fresh thyme leaves (optional). Pass the extra walnut topping at the table.

TOFU FRIED RICE

Tanya Whitlock
Home Chef
Cleveland, OH
Instagram: @myadventuresinveganism

" My husband is a vegan (most of the time, no judgment here!) and we do a lot of cooking together. This quick and easy meal is a favorite of ours. It's ideal for meal prepping work lunches—make a big batch, then divide it into five small servings.

Use extra firm tofu, putting it between two plates with a cast iron skillet (or something else heavy) on top to drain the excess fluid before you cube and cook. You can do this while you chop the other ingredients to save time."

Serves 4

INGREDIENTS

1 package of extra firm tofu, drained and cubed

2 tablespoons sesame oil

1 cup peas

1 cup shredded carrot

1/4 cup chopped green onion

2 teaspoons minced ginger

1 teaspoon minced garlic

Soy sauce to taste (start with 2 tablespoons)

4 cups cooked rice of choice

Green onions for garnish

INSTRUCTIONS

Cook the rice according to directions, set aside.

Sauté tofu cubes on medium heat in the sesame oil until lightly brown.

Add soy sauce and toss.

Stir in shredded carrots, peas, garlic, and ginger, and sauté for 5 minutes.

Add rice and toss for another 5 minutes on medium heat.

Top with green onion and serve.

 RBVK Tip: Is your tofu falling apart in your stir-fry, even when you press it? Try freezing it. Freezing tofu and then defrosting when ready to use makes the texture firmer and chewier by removing more of the moisture. Buy a few packages at once, drain and press, then cube (or cut into slices) and freeze so you'll have it on hand quickly for future dishes. You can also marinate the tofu before you freeze it to make it even more "ready-to-go" (to add to salads and sandwiches). When ready to use, defrosting in a microwave makes it even chewier.

HUNGARIAN PAPRIKASH

Meredith Pangrace
Home Chef
Cleveland, OH

" This is the recipe that gave me the idea for this book. My family has a tradition of gathering for New Year's Day dinner. We eat the traditional sauerkraut for good luck, along with other Eastern European family favorites. During the pandemic of 2020, our family pod was small, but we still wanted to gather to do something special. I decided to make the traditional dinner completely vegan as a challenge. While I had made other versions of traditional food over the years, this was my first time attempting a paprikash.

This version uses Butler Soy Curls (see "Pantry Staples," p. 16) as the replacement for shredded chicken. If you can't find them, you can use a frozen shredded chicken substitute (Gardein or Morning Star Farms brand). Or simply double the amount of mushrooms.

I like paprikash served over egg noodles. There are some egg-free "ribbon noodles," often in the kosher section, but actually, Walmart's house brand, Great Value, makes egg-free wide pasta ribbons that are the closest to real egg noodles I've found. You can really use any pasta that can stand up to the rich, thick sauce. Or you can serve over mashed potatoes. In 2020, I made the noodles, the potatoes, and the pierogies (see recipe on p. 110), because we all needed as much carb comfort as we could get that day.

This recipe makes a very large pot. You can halve the recipe or have leftovers to give to friends or freeze. It takes a bit of work, but your house will smell fantastic."

Serves 6–8

INGREDIENTS

3 cups Butler Soy Curls

1 cup cashews

2 cups of unsweetened plant milk

1 tablespoon apple cider vinegar

Salt and pepper

4 teaspoons salt

1 teaspoon black pepper

2 teaspoons onion powder

2 teaspoons garlic powder

1 teaspoon of nutmeg

4 tablespoons sweet paprika

4 tablespoons smoked paprika

2 tablespoons olive oil

2 onions, diced

2 red bell peppers, diced

16 ounces white mushrooms, sliced

2 tablespoons soy sauce

2 tablespoons chopped fresh garlic

3 tablespoons tomato paste

4 tablespoons flour

2 cans diced tomatoes, drained

3 cups vegetable broth

2 teaspoons white vinegar

1/2 teaspoon baking soda

cooked noodles or mashed potatoes parsley to garnish

INSTRUCTIONS

Place the soy curls in a large bowl. Place the cashews in a second large bowl.

Boil a pot of water. Pour boiling water over the cashews and the soy curls to cover. Let the cashews soak and soften, and let the soy curls rehydrate for about 15 minutes.

Prepare and measure out all your spices (ingredients listed from salt to paprika) into one small bowl while you're waiting so they are ready to go when you need them.

Drain the soy curls and squeeze out the water. Toss with a pinch of salt and pepper and set aside.

Drain and rinse the cashews. Add them to a blender with plant milk, 1 tablespoon of apple cider vinegar, and a pinch of salt and pepper. Blend until smooth and set aside.

In a large pot, add your olive oil. When hot, add the onions and red bell pepper and sauté over medium-high heat until the onions are translucent.

Add the sliced mushrooms and soy sauce and continue cooking until the mushrooms release their water. Add the garlic and sauté another minute or two.

Push the mushrooms and veggies to the side. Add the tomato paste and flour, stirring constantly to make a sauce-thickening paste. Slowly whisk in the broth.

Add the white vinegar and baking soda. Stir to combine, then incorporate the sauce into the vegetables.

Bring to a boil, then immediately lower to a simmer.

Add the cashew cream to the pot.

Add the hydrated soy curls. Simmer for at least 30 minutes for the flavors to incorporate. The longer you simmer on low, the better the flavors will be.

Spoon over the noodles or potataoes to serve, and garnish with parsley.

PRAKES (STUFFED CABBAGE)

Beth Segal
Home Chef | Food Writer and Photographer
Cleveland, OH

" According to Wikipedia, there are forty-two distinct names for stuffed cabbage. From Sweden to Japan to the Dominican Republic, that's an international smorgasbord of at least a thousand culinary variations. Even to discuss this one iteration would take more space than it's entitled to. The insatiably curious can consult Volume III of the *Language and Culture Atlas of Ashkenazic Jewry* for the linguistic map of Yiddish terms for stuffed cabbage; everyone else can just proceed to this version of my family's well-loved recipe, a relatively rare meatless variation of the Romanian/Moldavian/Southern Ukranian version of the universally embraced dish."

Makes 18–22 prakes

INGREDIENTS

1 head green cabbage (2–2 1/2 pounds)

3 cups white or yellow onions, thinly sliced

2 tablespoons olive oil

1 tablespoon brown sugar

2 tablespoons lemon juice

1 teaspoon grated lemon peel

1/2 teaspoon cinnamon, divided

1 1/2 cups raisins

2 tablespoons tomato paste

1 28-ounce can crushed tomatoes

2 tablespoons Bob's Red Mill Egg Replacer

4 tablespoons water

1 1/2 cups grated onions

1 cup white long-grain rice, boiled for 6 minutes and drained

Salt and pepper to taste

INSTRUCTIONS

Freeze cabbage overnight. This will break down the leaves and make them pliable for cooking. In the morning, defrost the cabbage, and peel off the perfectly soft leaves, one by one, and set aside. Shave off any of the big ribs with a sharp small knife. If some the leaves are really big, cut in half. The small leaves just before the core can be shredded and sautéed with the onions below.

Preheat the oven to 300°F.

In a large skillet over low heat, slowly cook the sliced onions (and any shredded cabbage) in the olive oil until they are soft but not brown. Add sugar, lemon juice and peel, cinnamon, one half of the raisins, tomato paste, and crushed tomatoes. Stir and simmer for 20 minutes, stirring occasionally.

In a separate bowl, mix the egg replacer and water and let sit for 1 minute. Mix well and add the grated onions, rice, remaining cinnamon, and raisins. Place a spoonful or two of this mixture on each cabbage leaf. Tuck in the ends and fold the leaves over to completely encase the filling, like a small burrito.

Place the stuffed cabbage in the skillet with the sauce. Cover and cook for about 25 minutes.

 RBVK Tip: One of our favorite ways to make stuffed cabbage a meal is to serve it with mashed potatoes—with the extra tomato sauce ladled on top.

Once you get comfortable with assembling stuffed cabbages, experiment with your own fillings and sauces to add to those thousands of variations! My family likes lentils, chopped walnuts, and mushrooms for a filling. Our grandmother's secret sauce consisted simply of Campbell's Condensed Tomato Soup—easy but still so delicious!

DUMPLINGS WITH GRAVY

Gretchen Vandenberghe
Home Chef
Monroe, MI

" My whole family went vegan after watching a documentary about the meat industry. I have been adapting some of our favorite recipes as well as trying new ones. This recipe is an adaptation of a longtime family favorite. It is comfort in a bowl! If you can't find Ocean Halo NoChicken Broth you can substitute Better Than Bouillon Vegetarian No Chicken Base or your favorite vegetable broth."

Serves 4-6

INGREDIENTS

Chickpea gravy:

1/2 cup onion, small diced

1/2 cup celery, small diced

2 cloves garlic, minced

1/4 cup vegan butter (I use Earth Balance sticks)

1/2 cup flour

2 teaspoons sugar

1 teaspoon salt

1 teaspoon dried basil

1/2 teaspoon ground black pepper

4 cups vegan no chicken broth (I use Ocean Halo)

1 12-ounce bag frozen green peas

1 15-ounce can chickpeas, drained and rinsed

Dumplings:

2 cups Bisquick

2 teaspoons dried basil

2/3 cup plant milk (I use almond or soy)

INSTRUCTIONS

Preheat oven to 350°F.

In a large skillet, melt butter on medium-high heat. Add onion and celery and sauté until they are translucent.

Add garlic, stir for 1 minute.

Slowly add the flour. Turn heat down to medium and stir mixture continuously for about 1 minute.

Add sugar, salt, basil, and pepper. Add the broth, one cup at a time, whisking to avoid clumps. Bring to a boil, stirring constantly until mixture becomes thick like gravy, then reduce the heat to medium.

Add the chickpeas and frozen peas.

Pour into a 13 x 9-inch baking dish. Set aside.

For the biscuits: In a small bowl, mix together Bisquick, basil, and plant milk with a fork. Mix until moist, don't overmix.

Drop spoonfuls of dumpling mixture on top of chickpea mixture. You should have about 12 dumplings.

Bake uncovered for 30 minutes. Then cover with tin foil tightly and bake an additional 10 minutes. Remove from the oven and let cool a bit before serving. Gravy will thicken as it cools.

SHEPHERD'S PIE

Josh Ingram
Professional Chef | GO Buddha
Rocky River, OH
gobuddhameals.com
Instagram: @gobuddhameals

" I am the founder of GO Buddha (a vegan, gluten-free cafe and meal prep service), which has curated thousands of affordable plant-based meals. Our mission is to disrupt the current food system by creating a more accessible and sustainable meal service, inspiring healthy families, and supporting stronger communities.

This recipe is comforting, soulful, and a little bit humbling. These are the simple dishes that make us realize that we don't need much in this world to be happy. Good food and a healthy, happy family."

Serves 6

INGREDIENTS

For the filling:
1 1/2 pounds portabella mushrooms, chopped
1 onion, diced
2 large carrots, diced
3 stalks celery, diced
2 cloves garlic, minced
6 ounces green beans, blanched and bias cut
1 tablespoon tomato paste
1/4 teaspoon fresh thyme
1/2 teaspoon paprika
3/4 cup to 1 cup vegetable broth
Pinch of red pepper flakes
Salt and pepper to taste

For the mashed potatoes:

3 large russet potatoes peeled and cubed

Cold water as needed

1 cup oat milk

1 clove garlic, minced

Salt and pepper as needed

2 tablespoons olive oil

INSTRUCTIONS

Preheat the oven to 400°F.

Heat a sauté pan over medium-high heat. Add the mushrooms and cook 3–4 minutes until the mushrooms have begun to brown.

Add the onions, celery, and carrots. Season with salt, pepper, paprika, thyme, and red pepper flakes. Cook 4–5 minutes until the vegetables are soft and slightly caramelized. Add the tomato paste, distributing throughout the pan.

Reduce the heat to medium, add the garlic, and cook until fragrant (about 45 seconds). Add the green beans and 1/4 cup of the stock, stirring to combine. Taste and adjust seasonings as needed.

Add the potatoes to a large pot and cover with cold water by 2 inches. Add a generous pinch of salt and boil for 10–12 minutes until the potatoes are fork tender. As the potatoes are cooking, add the oat milk, garlic, and olive oil to a small saucepan. Heat until the liquid is hot to the touch.

Drain the potatoes and return to the pot. Mash the potatoes while slowly adding the oat milk mixture. Mash until desired consistency is achieved.

When ready to assemble, transfer the filling to a 9 x 9-inch baking dish or 12-inch round dish. Spoon the mashed potatoes on top of the filling and spread evenly, smoothing the top with the back of a spatula or spoon. If desired, use a fork to create a swirl pattern in the potatoes. Dot with more butter (if desired, or brush with olive oil) and bake 30 minutes, then broil for 5 minutes until the potatoes are golden brown.

PARTY FOOD!

SPINACH & ARTICHOKE DIP

Lauren Spisak
Home Chef
Cleveland, OH
Facebook: @yeahthatvegansh1t
Instagram: @VeganinCleveland

" I've been interested in animals and animal welfare for a long time, so veganism just seemed like a logical step. Back when I first became vegan, I started a recipe blog called *Yeah, That Vegan Shit* to motivate myself to cook and try new recipes and to find some community with other vegans—the blog's still around but has since moved to Facebook. I also started a blog called *Vegan in Cleveland* to help vegans locate vegan food in the Cleveland area, back when it wasn't as easily accessible. The blog lives on in a Facebook page where I regularly post my favorite vegan food from local restaurants.

One of my favorite things about cooking and sharing vegan recipes is being able to challenge people's misconceptions about the boringness/flavorlessness of vegan food and winning that 'oh my god, this is vegan??' reaction. This recipe is one that regularly earns that response."

Serves 4

INGREDIENTS

1 (15 1/2-ounce) can Great Northern beans, drained

1 tablespoon olive oil

1 small onion, diced

5 cloves garlic, minced

4 cups fresh spinach, torn into small pieces

1 (14 1/3-ounce) can artichoke hearts (quartered or whole is fine), drained and roughly chopped

1 tub of vegan cream cheese (I like the Tofutti brand, it's usually the easiest to find)

1/4 cup panko bread crumbs

2 tablespoons nutritional yeast

1/2 teaspoon sea salt

Pepper (to taste)

INSTRUCTIONS

Preheat the oven to 400°F.

Heat the olive oil on medium heat in a pan. Add onion with a pinch of salt and cook until nearly translucent. Add garlic and cook 1 minute more. Toss in your spinach and cook until wilted (2–3 minutes). Remove from heat.

Toss your drained beans into a food processor along with the tub of vegan cream cheese and puree until mostly smoothed. Add chopped artichoke hearts and pulse until mixed in.

Transfer to a mixing bowl and add spinach/onion/garlic mix, 2 tablespoons panko, and nutritional yeast. Mix well.

Transfer to a casserole dish (I prefer a bit wider and shallower dish rather than deep and stout, although both work in a pinch). Sprinkle remaining panko on top.

Cover with lid or foil and cook for about 20 minutes.

Remove lid/foil and cook for 10 or 15 minutes more, until a little browned and heated through.

Let sit at least 15–20 minutes before serving.

SWEET & SPICY PARTY BALLS

Maura Schroeder
Home Chef
Cleveland, OH

" No one needs to know how easy these are to make. You can warm all the ingredients in a skillet, but I prefer to put everything in a Crock-Pot to heat, then drop to low to serve warm. Great for parties or tailgating. I made these for a Christmas party and my nephew called them 'balls of deliciousness!'"

Serves 6

INGREDIENTS

1 bag of frozen meatless meatballs
1 12-ounce bottle of chili sauce
1 1/2 cups grape jelly

INSTRUCTIONS

In a skillet on medium heat, combine chili sauce, jelly, and meatballs until hot.

Simmer until the sauce thickens. Serve with toothpicks.

SAUERKRAUT BALLS

Meredith Pangrace
Home Chef
Cleveland, OH

> My heart has been broken far too many times by biting into a sauerkraut ball promised to be vegetarian, only to find a sneaky chunk of meat. Never again!"

Serves 4

INGREDIENTS

16 ounces sauerkraut, well-drained

3 green onions, just the tops

3/4 cup crumbled vegan sausage (I like Field Roast links)

1/3 cup vegan cream cheese (I like Kite Hill)

1 tablespoon horseradish mustard (or regular mustard with 1 teaspoon horseradish)

1/8 teaspoon black pepper

2 tablespoons panko

1 tablespoon nutritional yeast

For the breading:

Vegetable oil, enough for frying

1 cup flour

1 1/2 cups panko bread crumbs

2 flax eggs (2 tablespoons ground flax and 6 tablespoons water—mix and let rest a few minutes)

1/2 cup German beer

For the dipping sauce:

1 cup vegan mayo

1 1/2 tablespoons horseradish mustard

Black pepper to taste

1 tablespoon fresh parsley for garnish

INSTRUCTIONS

In a large bowl, mix the first 8 ingredients with your hands and put in the freezer to chill and firm up for 30 minutes.

Make the dipping sauce while waiting by combining the ingredients and adjusting to taste.

Prepare your fry station by heating vegetable oil in a pan on the stove to about 400°F. You'll want enough oil in your pan for the balls to be about halfway submerged, so the amount of oil you need depends on your pan.

While the oil is heating up, put your flax eggs into a bowl and whisk in the beer.

Pour the flour onto one plate. Pour the panko onto a separate plate.

Take the sauerkraut mixture out of the freezer. The cream cheese should hold the balls together pretty well.

Use a cookie scoop, a spoon, or your hands to make a 1-inch ball of the kraut mixture. Dredge the ball first in flour, then your beer mixture, then the panko.

Add to the oil carefully. Continue shaping the balls, breading, and adding to the oil until the pan is full. Watch the balls carefully and flip with a fork when brown and crispy, about 2 minutes each side. You may have to do this in batches, depending on the size of your pan. You don't want the balls to be too crowded.

Drain on a cooling rack over a cookie sheet.

To serve, sprinkle with the fresh parsley and the dipping sauce.

CHICAGO-STYLE DEEP-DISH PIZZA

Tiffany Wilson

Professional Chef | Feed Your Head
Chicago, IL
feedyourheadfoods.com
Facebook: @feedyourheadchicago
Instagram: @feedyourheadchicago
Twitter: @feedyourheadveg

"Established in 2011, Feed Your Head is dedicated to creating delicious vegan cheeses and faux meats using a handcrafted, small-batch process. We take fresh, seasonal ingredients characteristic of the Midwest and purchased from as many local farmers and purveyors as possible. With minimal ingredients and zero preservatives, our products are packed with flavor and are 100 percent vegan. We began by selling products at Chicago farmers markets and summer music festivals. It wasn't long after dabbling in vegan cheeses that I delved into making vegan meat. My deep ties to food and traditional culinary practices, derived from my rural Missouri roots, lend a great deal of passion to my business and my desire to support local farms. For me, it's about introducing others to the idea that vegan food can be delicious on its own merits.

Chef's Note: If you don't use the sauce recipe provided, just make sure the sauce you use is nice and chunky!

Makes one large pizza (8 slices)

INGREDIENTS

You'll need a deep-dish pizza pan for this, lightly oiled

For the dough:

1 1/2 cups warm water

1 1/2 teaspoons sugar

1 tablespoon yeast

1 tablespoon salt

1 tablespoon extra-virgin olive oil

3 cups flour

For the sauce:

1 15-ounce can crushed tomatoes

1 15-ounce can diced tomatoes

1 tablespoon extra-virgin olive oil

1/2 onion, chopped

1/2–3/4 teaspoon salt

1 teaspoon basil, chopped

1/4 teaspoon oregano

2 cloves garlic, minced

Toppings:

1 package Feed Your Head cashew Mozzarella

1 package Feed Your Head pepperoni

1 package Feed Your Head Italian sausage

1 onion, chopped

1 bell pepper, chopped

INSTRUCTIONS

To make the dough (makes 32 ounces of dough):

Dissolve sugar in water, sprinkle yeast, and let sit 10 minutes.

Mix salt and olive oil into water/yeast/sugar mixture.

Add flour.

Knead for 10 minutes.

Cover with a towel and let it rest in a warm place for one hour.

Punch down the dough and let sit for another 45 minutes.

To make the sauce:

Cook onions in olive oil for 5–7 minutes

Add garlic, basil, and oregano and stir.

Add tomatoes and salt.

Bring to a boil, reduce heat, and simmer for 15 minutes.

To assemble:

Preheat oven to 420°F.

Spread the dough evenly in deep-dish pan, making sure the sides are a little raised on the pan.

Grate the mozzarella onto the base of the crust.

Add the pepperoni, onions, bell peppers, and sausage.

Top with pizza sauce.

Bake on the bottom rack for 46 minutes. Let cool for 20 minutes before slicing.

BACKYARD BOUNTY
POTATO SALAD

Kelly Neef
Home Chef | Green Patch Garden
Mansfield, OH
greenpatchgarden.com

"I am a lifelong vegan and Rust Belt native who grows and sells certified organic vegetable plants with my family. Our small greenhouse operation, Green Patch Garden, is based in Mansfield, Ohio. We focus on heirloom vegetable varieties with an emphasis on biodiversity and sustainable practices. Our mission is to inspire, educate, and encourage better food choices for an enhanced quality of life through backyard gardening and local food chains. We believe we can improve the quality of our lives through the quality of our food, soil, and sustainability of our environment.

Nothing says Rust Belt quite like potatoes. And when paired with kale, the poster child of veganism, you have something very comforting and nourishing. This recipe is a showcase for the flavor our backyard gardens can offer. What I really love is how versatile and simple this recipe is, while still bringing the flavor. Feel free to experiment with whatever fresh vegetables you have on hand. Play with the potato-kale ratio (I have made this with just kale and just potatoes—still yummy). You can use 1-2 teaspoons of your favorite vinegar in place of lemon. Also consider adding any fresh herbs you may have grown or bought from the farmers market; dill, parsley, oregano, or basil."

Chef's note: I highly recommend growing your own tomatoes, purchasing them from a farmers market, or begging from a gardener-friend. Grocery store tomatoes may look pretty, but they are grown to resist bruising and have a long shelf life. They are often picked green and artificially ripened with gas. If you can't get your hands on a good tomato, omit them from the recipe and replace them with another vegetable, plus a teaspoon or two more of lemon juice or vinegar to compensate for lost juice and acidity.

144

RUST BELT VEGAN KITCHEN

Serves 8

INGREDIENTS

1 pound small potatoes (red, fingerling, or gold), unpeeled and quartered

1 small cucumber, peeled and diced

1 large colorful bell pepper, or similar amount of sweet Italian peppers, diced

1 medium-large fresh garden tomato, diced

2–3 large kale leaves, deveined and chopped into bite-size pieces

3 tablespoons tahini

3 tablespoons sliced Kalmata olives or dill pickles

Juice from half of a small lemon

1 1/2 teaspoons salt

1 teaspoon cumin

Pepper to taste

INSTRUCTIONS

Boil the quartered potatoes in a large stockpot until easily poked with a fork, about 10 minutes. Strain and set aside to cool.

Meanwhile, mix your prepped veggies (cucumber, pepper, tomato) and olives or pickles (or both!) with the tahini, lemon, salt, cumin, and pepper in a large salad bowl. The juice from the tomatoes will mingle with the lemon and tahini to form a creamy dressing. Taste and adjust the seasoning to your liking.

Add the completely cooled potatoes and stir until coated with dressing.

Finally, being the gentle lover you are, squeeze (massage!) the kale in your hands a few times to increase tenderness. Add to the salad bowl and mix. Taste and add more salt, pepper, lemon, or cumin to your liking.

CLASSIC HUMMUS

Michael Koury
Home Chef
Cleveland, OH

" This hummus recipe is my 'go to' for dinner party appetizers, movie night, or a simple side dish. The recipe is a variation of many different recipes from my mother and Lebanese family, perfected with the best of all the ideas. It's a simple, healthy, fresh dish with flavor and authenticity."

Serves 4-6

INGREDIENTS

2 15 1/2-ounce cans of chickpeas

1 heaping tablespoon of tahini

3 tablespoons olive oil

3 tablespoons fresh lemon juice

4 Kalamata olives

Garlic powder to taste

Salt to taste

Pepper to taste

INSTRUCTIONS

Drain and discard water from 1 can of beans. Do not drain the second can.

Pour 1/2 of the can of the drained beans into a blender.

Slowly add the olive oil.

Blend in a food processor or high-powered blender to a chunky mix.

Add tahini.

Add just the water from the second can of beans to the mixture.

Blend until smooth.

Add remaining beans from the first can and blend.

Slowly add remaining can of beans while blending.

Add lemon juice, garlic powder, salt, and pepper.

Blend until smooth. Consistency should be thick but not chunky.

Scoop hummus onto a plate, drizzle with olive oil, and garnish with olives.

 RBVK Tip: Our test kitchen says, "I loved this hummus! I had some store-bought garlic hummus to compare it to, and this one is hands-down better."

PICKLETINI

Abby Lesniak and Lauryn Swanger
Professional Chefs | Bold Pickin's Specialty Pickles
Cleveland, OH
Facebook: @boldpickinsspecialtypickles
Instagram: @boldpickins

> We started our company, Bold Pickin's Specialty Pickles, in 2018. We started out with a passion for gardening and cooking, and with a LOT of cucumbers. Sick of the same old boring pickle recipes, we reimagined them into the bold flavors contained in each of our jars.
>
> We created this drink for a New Year's Eve party."

Makes 1 cocktail

INGREDIENTS

2 1/2 ounces vodka

1/2 ounce dry vermouth

1 ounce pickle juice (Bold Pickin's Butter My Bread)

1 pickled jalapeno (for garnish)

INSTRUCTIONS

Fill a cocktail shaker with 4–5 ice cubes.

Add vodka, dry vermouth, and pickle juice.

Shake vigorously.

Pour into martini glass and garnish with pickled jalapeno.

DESSERTS

KMISH BREAD

Shelley Segal
Home Chef
Minneapolis, MN

" I grew up eating my mother's kmish bread in Minnesota. It was good, but as a kid, there were other, gooier cookies that she made that I liked better. When I grew up and moved to New York City and started frequenting the bakeries that are seemingly on every corner, there was inevitably a glass jar on the counter filled with what looked exactly like my mother's kmish bread, but it was called biscotti and was selling for $3 a piece. Gobsmacked is putting it lightly. Turns out my mother had been making the Yiddish version of these elegant Italian cookies all those years and I just wanted the snickerdoodles. Anyway, my taste has finally come around to the non-gooey, but I still prefer my mother's kmish bread to anybody's biscotti."—*Beth, daughter of Shelley*

Chef's notes: You need to chill the dough overnight in the refrigerator, so plan accordingly. These keep well if stored in a sealed container and are a good emergency cookie as they can be frozen for months, well-packaged, without consequence.

Makes 14–16 slices

INGREDIENTS

1 cup sugar

1/4 cup vegetable or canola oil

2 teaspoons vanilla

3 tablespoons Bob's Red Mill Egg Replacer

6 tablespoons water

3 cups flour

2 teaspoons baking powder

2 teaspoons cinnamon

1/2 teaspoon salt

2 cups chopped pecans

1 generous cup chopped best dark chocolate chips (many dark chocolate chips are vegan, but check the ingredients for milk fat)

INSTRUCTIONS

Mix together the sugar, oil, and vanilla in the bowl of a stand mixer.

In a separate bowl, combine the egg replacer and water. Let sit for one minute, stir, and add to the sugar mixture. Mix well.

Combine the flour, baking powder, cinnamon, and salt in a separate bowl and then add to the wet ingredients. Mix only until ingredients are combined (making sure to incorporate all the flour mix). Refrigerate overnight.

In the morning, preheat the oven to 300°F. Form the batter into 5 or 6 long rolls, about 10 inches long and 3 inches wide. Flatten slightly and then bake for about 25–35 minutes, or until golden on the bottom.

Let cool completely and then cut diagonally into 1/2-inch slices. Sprinkle lightly with a little more cinnamon if desired.

Bake again for 7–10 minutes until light golden brown. Cool completely before serving.

BUCKEYE BARS

Bonnie Tawse
Home Chef | Cookbook Author
Chicago, IL

"   When I was recipe testing for *The Belt Cookie Table Cookbook*, it was peak pandemic lockdown and the world was teeming with uncertainty. When I tested a classic Ohio buckeye recipe, I asked my teenage son to help me make them. He's not that interested in baking, but he adores the combination of chocolate and peanut butter, so I figured it would lift his spirits. With traditional buckeyes, you roll the peanut butter mixture in a ball and then dip it in melted chocolate. But the recipe didn't state that you need to chill the peanut butter mixture before you dip them. So as we were dipping the warmish peanut butter balls in the melted chocolate, they were coming apart and losing their uniform round shapes, and they looked absolutely nothing like buckeyes. Rather than getting dismayed, we both just started cracking up at the supreme mess we were making and how pathetic our confections looked. It was the first time we had both laughed that hard in months and for that, I was grateful. I figured out that there was a missing step in the recipe and we proceeded (after a 30-minute chill in the freezer) to make pretty decent-looking buckeyes, but honestly, the first-round 'mistakes' were just as tasty. A few months later, I decided it might be a tad easier, quicker, and less messy to just take the same ingredients and make them into bars. Also, these are a no-bake confection, so they're good when you don't want to heat up the kitchen. My teenager gives these two enthusiastic thumbs up."

Makes about 16 bars

INGREDIENTS

3/4 cup plant-based butter, melted

3 1/2 cups powdered sugar

1 16-ounce jar of creamy peanut butter

1 teaspoon pure vanilla extract

2 cups semisweet vegan chocolate chips (I like Guittard)

1 tablespoon plant-based butter

INSTRUCTIONS

Line a 9 x 13-inch baking dish with parchment paper, set aside.

In a large mixing bowl, beat the 3/4 cup melted vegan butter, powdered sugar, peanut butter, and vanilla. The ingredients will come together into a soft "dough." Scoop out into the baking dish and using a spatula or your hands, press the mixture into the bottom of the dish.

Put the chocolate chips and 1 tablespoon of vegan butter in a microwave-safe bowl. Heat in the microwave at 30-second intervals, taking out and stirring and returning it to the microwave. It should take about 3 or 4 times (about a minute and a half total) to melt the chocolate. Melt and stir until the chocolate is smooth.

Spoon the melted chocolate on top of the peanut butter layer and spread evenly across the entire surface.

Let the buckeye bars cool completely and set before slicing into squares. If it is warm, you can put the pan in the refrigerator to speed up the cooling. To get clean lines when cutting the bars, dip the knife in hot water and then wipe all the water off before slicing. These are rich, so I cut them into small squares or halve each square into two triangles.

COCONUT-LIME
PAWPAW PALETAS

Professional Chef | Cookbook Author
@sausagetarian
Marietta, OH

There are so many delicious wild edibles growing throughout the Rust Belt that subsiding mostly on plants is no challenge at all. Pawpaws, the largest fruit native to North America, are my favorite. So much so that I wrote an entire cookbook, *The Pocket Pawpaw Cookbook*, devoted to them.

The mango-pineapple-banana flavor of pawpaws works well in refreshing frozen treats, but you won't see pawpaw paletas in Mexico, as it's south of the tree's range. If you can't find pawpaws, try substituting mangos."

INGREDIENTS

11/4 cups pawpaw pulp

1/2 cup coconut milk, well-shaken

1/4 cup agave nectar

1/4 cup water

2 tablespoons lime juice

Pinch salt

INSTRUCTIONS

Combine all the ingredients in a blender and blend until smooth.

Divide between 6, 3-ounce ice pop molds and freeze overnight.

To unmold, run hot water over the mold for a few seconds.

Chef's Note: For spicy paletas, omit the salt and add some Tajín seasoning (look for it in the Latin section at stores) to the paleta base, or sprinkle it on the unmolded paletas when you serve them. For speckled paletas, stir a few tablespoons of chia seeds into the paleta base after pureeing.

RUST BELT VEGAN KITCHEN

CONCHAS

Oscar Narváez

Professional Chef | The Chunky Scone
Waukegan, Illinois
thechunkyscones.com
Facebook: @thechunkyscones
Instagram: @thechunkyscone

" Conchas are a soft and sweet Mexican bread with a white topping that resembles the surface of a seashell. They were part of my childhood. My parents used to drop me off at my grandma's when I was kid when they would go to work. At my grandma's house, we ate modestly, but there was so much love in spite of the lack of resources. My grandma grew up eating lots of bread since her grandfather was a baker. Her favorite pan dulce, or sweet bread, was conchas. When I would stay overnight at her house, she would bring me breakfast in bed on a tray with a concha, and that alone would make me the happiest of kids in my view. We often go back to the things that made us happy once, and this is true for me in this regard."

Makes 6 portions

INGREDIENTS

For the dough:

2 cups all-purpose flour (King Arthur preferred or any other flour with 4 grams or more of protein per 1/4 of a cup)

1/4 cup vegan sugar

1/2 teaspoon salt

1/2 teaspoon **instant** dry yeast (Make sure it is instant dry yeast and not active dry yeast. Instant dry yeast does not need to be activated before using and active dry yeast does.)

1 1/4 cup coconut milk

For the paste:

1/2 cup powdered sugar

1/2 cup all-purpose flour (same flour as for the dough)

2 tablespoons cocoa powder or peanut butter powder (whichever you prefer or both!)

3 tablespoons unmelted coconut oil (for measuring purposes make sure it is unmelted)

A Ziploc plastic bag cut into a rectangle about 6 x 4 inches, or a piece of plastic wrap this size

INSTRUCTIONS

Make the dough: In a clean mixing bowl, add all your dry ingredients and mix with a whisk until blended.

Add the coconut milk to the dry ingredients. Mix with a spatula.

Start working the dough with your hands, tossing it and bringing it back to the center of the bowl as if it was a basketball. The dough will be sticky, so be patient and keep tossing it, rolling it down to the middle of the bowl until the dough does not stick to your hands anymore. This process can take up to 10 minutes or more.

Shape the dough into a ball and let it rest, covered with a plastic bag or a wet kitchen towel for up to 2 hours or until it has doubled in size. (Room temperature is key for dough to rise faster, so anything above 70°F should be good.)

Once the dough has risen for 2 hours or doubled in size, take it out of the bowl and place it on a lightly floured, clean surface. Cut into 6 equal parts. Shape your 6 pieces of dough one by one into little balls by pressing it against the surface and rolling against it to give them a perfect round shape. (It doesn't have to be perfect, but do try your best. Make conchas every weekend for practice!)

Place your 6 round balls of dough on a baking tray and cover with a plastic bag or a wet towel so they do not dry out while you work on your paste for the top. While you work on your paste, your shaped dough will proof for about 20 minutes or so.

Preheat your oven to 350°F.

Make the paste: In a clean mixing bowl, place all your dry ingredients and mix with a whisk until fully combined.

Melt the coconut oil in a small pot over low heat until the oil is just lukewarm and is safe to touch.

Add your dry ingredients to the warm coconut oil.

Mix with a spatula first, then work the dough with your hands until the paste has the texture of Play-Doh and you can shape it into a form without it sticking to your hands. (If necessary, add a tiny bit more of oil, but do not make it too squishy because it will be harder to work with.)

Cut the paste into 6 equal pieces.

Place a ball of paste in the middle of the piece of plastic wrap or Ziploc bag you cut, and flatten it with a cutting board to press it into a flat, thin circle. Gently place the circle of paste on top of a ball of dough. It should be large enough to drape down the sides of the balls of dough. Repeat with the rest of the conchas.

Cut 5–6 scores on the top of the conchas with a knife. Concha means "shell" in Spanish, so imagine the lines on a shell, with a delicate curve. Or just be creative and score in any design you like.

Bake for 30 minutes or until golden brown. Let them cool off for 20 minutes or so and enjoy with a cup of coffee, tea, or hot chocolate.

MALTED BARLEY CAKE

Jessica Pinsky
Home Chef
Cleveland, OH

" Honey cake is a traditional cake for Rosh Hashanah, the Jewish New Year. We eat sweet foods on Rosh Hashanah as a way to celebrate a sweet new year ahead. This cake is traditionally the food used to break the fast of Rosh Hashanah: Jews will fast in observance of the holiday, and the first bite at sunset is sweet cake to bring a sweet new year. I love this vegan version, replacing honey with malted barley syrup. For me, it's a nod to my other favorite food—bagels!"

Chef's Note: If you prefer not to use the whiskey, you can omit it and replace the 1/4 cup liquid with additional orange juice or coffee. I usually make this in a 10-inch Bundt cake pan. Fill pan(s) 3/4 full to prevent spilling, as the cake will rise.

Serves 8

INGREDIENTS

3 1/2 cups all-purpose flour

1 tablespoon baking powder

1 teaspoon baking soda

1/2 teaspoon salt

4 teaspoons ground cinnamon

1/2 teaspoon ground cloves

1/4 teaspoon ground ginger

1/4 teaspoon nutmeg

1 cup vegetable oil

3/4 cup malted barley syrup

1 1/2 cups granulated sugar

1/2 cup brown sugar

3 flax eggs (3 tablespoons ground flax, 9 tablespoons water total)

1 teaspoon vanilla extract

1 cup brewed coffee

1/2 cup orange juice

1/4 cup rye whiskey

INSTRUCTIONS

Preheat the oven to 350°F. Lightly grease the pan(s).

In a large bowl, whisk together the flour, baking powder, baking soda, salt, and spices. Make a well in the center and add the oil, malted barley syrup, sugars, eggs, vanilla, coffee, orange juice, and rye whiskey (or substitute).

Using a strong wire whisk, and combine the ingredients to make a thick batter, making sure that no ingredients are stuck to the bottom of the bowl.

Pour the batter into the prepared pan(s) and sprinkle the top of the cake(s) evenly with the almonds.

Bake about 50 minutes. This may depend on what type of pan you use. This is a liquidy batter and, depending on your oven, it may need extra or less time. Cake should spring back when gently pressed and pull away slightly from the outside of the pan.

Let the cake stand for 15 minutes before removing it from the pan. Then invert it onto a wire rack to cool completely.

PUMPKIN CHEESECAKE

Dave Huffman

Professional Chef | Bitchy Vegan Homo
Cleveland, OH
bvhbakery.com
Instagram: @bitchyveganhomo

> " Looking for something to impress your dinner guests at the holidays or any other time of year? Look no further. This pumpkin cheesecake is a decadent treat that will have your guests wishing they would have left more room for dessert. In my pre-vegan days I loved the dairy- and egg-filled original, but now I know you don't need to rely on any animal products to create an amazing dessert."

Serves 8-10

INGREDIENTS

16 ounces vegan cream cheese

8 ounces silken tofu

1 cup canned pumpkin (not pumpkin pie filling)

2/3 cup brown sugar

1/4 cup white sugar

1/4 cup flour

1/4 cup aquafaba

1 teaspoon cinnamon

1/2 teaspoon ginger

1/2 teaspoon nutmeg

1/4 teaspoon allspice

For the crust:

14 sheets graham crackers

2 tablespoons margarine, melted

3 tablespoons soy milk

INSTRUCTIONS

Preheat the oven to 350°F.

Pulse the graham crackers in a food processor and then place the crumbs in a large bowl.

Add the melted margarine and soy milk and mix until combined.

Place the crumb mixture into the bottom of a 9-inch springform pan.

With a spoon, press the crumbs into an even crust. Bake for 10 minutes.

While the crust is baking, put the cream cheese, tofu, pumpkin, brown sugar, sugar, flour, aquafaba, and spices into a food processor. Blend until everything is smooth and creamy, scraping down the sides as needed.

Pour the cream cheese mixture into the prepared crust.

Place the springform pan on a large piece of foil and carefully wrap the foil up the sides, making sure it doesn't tear. (You need it to be watertight.) Place the springform pan in a jelly roll pan or other large baking pan and fill the pan with hot water about halfway up the sides.

Place the pan in the oven and bake for 80 minutes.

Allow the cheesecake to cool on a wire rack and then cover and place it in the refrigerator for at least 8 hours before serving.

SPICE CAKE

Maura Schroeder
Home Chef
Cleveland, OH

" I grew up on South Bass Island, and as a kid, we had limited access to fresh produce, dairy, and eggs in the winter. My mom would sometimes need to substitute shelf-stable items for fresh. I remember her making cakes with mayo! So substituting pumpkin for eggs and oil was not a new concept for me. Adding walnuts and carob chips to this cake is my personal favorite. Most boxed spice cake mixes are vegan, but read the ingredients to be sure. Add in what makes you happy!"

Serves 8–10

INGREDIENTS

1 box Betty Crocker spice cake mix

1 15-ounce can pumpkin puree

1 teaspoon vanilla

1 teaspoon pumpkin pie spice (or cinnamon)

1/2 cup walnuts and/or 1/2 cup carob chips (optional)

INSTRUCTIONS

Preheat oven to 350°F.

Spray a Bundt pan with cooking spray.

In a large mixing bowl, mix cake mix, vanilla, spice, and pumpkin.

Stir in walnuts and carob chips (add as little or as much as you like). Batter will be dense.

Spoon into the Bundt pan and bake for 50 minutes or until a toothpick comes out clean. If you're using a different type of pan, check the bake times on the box. You can also make muffins, also adjusting the bake time. Drizzle with melted carob.

RBVK Tip: Want frosting? Pillsbury Creamy Supreme Vanilla is vegan. Or make your own quick icing by whisking together 1/2 cup powdered sugar with 1 tablespoon plant-based milk (vanilla-flavored is good here) and drizzle. Make sure the cake is cooled before frosting.

KOLACKY/KOLACHE

Meredith Pangrace
Home Chef
Cleveland, OH

" I've struggled to imagine a dough that would mimic the egg yolk and sour cream base of my grandma's perfect kolacky. But the answer was there in front of me all along. Rather than the traditional kolacky fold—square with just the corners tucked in, filling still exposed—she cuts hers into a triangle shape, fills, then rolls into a *crescent*.

Not long ago, I was listening to the podcast *Teaching Jasmine to Cook Vegan* when a guest shocked host Jasmine Singer by revealing that Pillsbury Crescent Rolls were vegan. There it was! While this is not an exact replica of my grandmother's kolacky, the dough is a solid way to deliver her perfect nut filling, which is really the star of the show. And I think she would appreciate the practicality of it."

INGREDIENTS

2 cans of Pillsbury Crescent Roll dough

1/2 cup powdered sugar

1/2 cup sugar

For the filling:

3 cups ground walnuts

1 cup brown sugar

1/2 cup white sugar

1/2 cup oat milk

INSTRUCTIONS

Preheat the oven to 375°F.

In a pan on the stove, mix the walnuts and sugar over medium heat and stir with a wooden spoon. Keep moving them around so they don't burn.

Slowly add the oat milk a little at a time and keep stirring. As the nuts cook and the sugar melts, the mixture will become like a paste. Keep mixing until the mixture starts to sizzle and bubble, then remove from the stove.

Spread the nut mixture out onto a plate and let cool.

Prepare your work surface for assembly: mix the powdered sugar and the granulated sugar. Sprinkle a handful of the mixture over your work area. You're going to assemble the kolacky on this mixture instead of on a floured surface. This is to sweeten the dough and to get the bottoms caramelized.

Take the dough out of the fridge. Take apart the perforated triangles. On the short side of each triangle, put a small scoop of the nut mixture. Roll up into a crescent shape, tucking in the sides. You don't want the filling to leak out when baking, so pinch the dough around the filling the best you can. It'll probably take a little experimenting to master exactly how much filling goes into each cookie. You want plenty of that delicious filling in each bite but want to avoid exploding kolacky.

After the pastries are rolled, press the bottom (point-side down) into the powdered sugar/white sugar mixture just to make sure the bottoms get enough on them.

Bake 13–15 minutes, watching carefully not to burn the bottom, until the tops are golden. Sprinkle with powdered sugar when cool.

 RBVK Tip: Extra filling stores well in the freezer. If the shaping of the kolacky is a little too challenging, you can also try rolling out the can of dough into one long piece (sealing the perforations), spreading the nut mixture down one side, and rolling like a strudel. Bake and slice.

RECIPE INDEX

THANK-YOUS

Thank you to all the chefs that contributed recipes to this book. Your creativity and enthusiam is truly inspiring. Thank you for sharing your culinarty talents in the spirit of this community.

Thank you to my Belt family—Anne, Martha, Michael, Dan, David, Bill, and Jim—for giving me the opportunity to put this book together. I love making books with you all.

Thank you to all the recipe testers and the Sunday Weenie Roast team: Marc, Sarah, Katie, Cheryl, Maura, Jessica, Michael, Brian, Matt, Beth, Danielle, Monica, Don, Ruth, Shelley, Hedy, and Sue.

Thank you to my friends, Beth and Elaine, whose brains I picked and advice I treasured in making this book, and to my fellow Belt cookbook editor Bonnie for the encouragement when I felt overwhelmed.

Thank you to my family—John, Ruth, Martin, Nate, Holly, and Scott—for your support and ecouragement in all the weird stuff I do, and for always eating whatever I have put in front of you over the years. Thank you to Sophie and Isabel for the Google docs training and for baking me the best vegan cupcakes ever for my birthday.

And finally, thank you readers! Please join the community on Instagram @rustbeltvegankitchen. I'd love to see what you're whipping up.